Contents

The
Principles
of
Smart
Development

Overview

This report provides guidance to communities in determining whether their local codes and standards encourage, support, or impede smart development. It also aims to help readers identify whether smart development principles and ideas fit their communities.

This report describes a development approach that adheres to the following principles:

1. Efficient Use of Land Resources

2. Full Use of Urban Services

3. Mixed Use

4. Transportation Options

5. Detailed, Human-Scale Design

6. Implementation

The first five principles, originally outlined by Livable Oregon, Inc., are "smart" ways of building a community, providing numerous benefits to all citizens. Development incorporating these principles conserves valuable land, energy, and facilities resources; offers people multiple convenient transportation options; relieves traffic congestion and air pollution; offers residents a variety of dwelling choices; and creates attractive community-oriented neighborhoods. The sixth principle, implementation, is, of course, essential to success.

This report provides guidance to communities in determining whether their local codes and standards encourage, support, or impede smart development. It also aims to help readers identify whether smart development principles and ideas fit their communities, and if smart development ideas would help to achieve local goals or meet state planning requirements.

Chapter 1 of this report outlines the principles of smart development, some of which may already be familiar to readers. Chapter 2 offers examples of two developments in Oregon communities that were able to incorporate a variety of these principles in their design after working with the community to implement them. Chapter 3 discusses the obstacles to smart development principles. Chapter 4 provides a series of strategies related to the principles, details the obstacles to implementing those strategies, and suggests solutions to dealing with those obstacles. Chapter 5 recommends a work program for the community that wants to change its development process to make it easier to implement these principles. Finally, the report includes two appendices. Appendix A offers a report from Livable Oregon, Inc., that summarizes the findings of a 1996 smart development symposium in Oregon. Appendix B uses language from the ordinances and plans of governments across the country to show how some communities are already implementing the strategies outlined in Chapter 4.

Not all of the strategies suggested here will be appropriate for all communities. Nevertheless, planners, planning commissioners, developers, neighborhood activists, and elected officials should consider using smart development strategies at appropriate times, such as during periodic review, development of master or specific plans, or in response to requests for individual plan or code amendments.

Smart development is neither unusual, nor is it particularly new. In addition to existing development patterns that subscribe to smart development principles, an increasing number of new projects employing these principles can be found throughout the United States.

Smart Development's Past

Most of the attributes of smart development can be found in older, pre-1950 American neighborhoods, many of which have held their value over decades as preferred places to live. These neighborhoods are laboratories of walkable, compact, mixed-use development.

Most of the attributes of smart development can be found in older, pre-1950 American neighborhoods, many of which have held their value over decades as preferred places to live. These neighborhoods are laboratories of walkable, compact, mixed-use development. In the first half of this century, American cities and towns were substantially different in their design. Street networks with small blocks connected neighborhood to neighborhood. Detached and attached housing often stood next to or within a block of each other. Local commercial services and parks were dispersed within or at the edges of neighborhoods. The basic compatibility of building types allowed for easy proximity of diverse uses and densities. Buildings were designed to contribute to a harmonious streetscape, and parking played a secondary role. Planning, engineering, regulatory, financial, building, and market systems worked together to allow and encourage this style of development.

Around 1950, the country experienced a fundamental change in the built landscape, a shift driven by new demographics, new economics, and the rise of the automobile. Separated, single-use developments became the custom. Street patterns became disconnected, typified by the dead-end cul-de-sac. Stand-alone office parks, shopping centers, recreation centers, apartment complexes, and single-family tract housing developments defined the newer American landscape. Different building types no longer shared proximity, so compatibility no longer mattered. As an example, the corner store, which functions compatibly within a neighborhood, evolved into the auto-oriented convenience store located on a commercial strip.

Gradually, standard subdivision and zoning practices have changed to accommodate this kind of development, and the financial, regulatory, and building industries have become almost exclusively focused on separate-use projects. As a result, financing and approval processes for these kind of conventional projects are relatively straightforward and low risk.

Smart development projects run into difficulty because they draw on lessons learned from older neighborhoods, on a style of building that

Smart development supports face-to-face, informal meeting between people—a fundamental aspect of community building.

has been largely forgotten for the last 40 years. These projects sometimes clash with convention, facing procedural problems that make them more difficult to build.

Who Might Initiate Change?

Change can start from a number of sources: a developer of a subdivision might suggest a new way to address land partitioning; a planner or planning commissioner might return from a conference where mixed uses were discussed and seek to apply the ideas to some of the community's neighborhood centers; or an elected official might want to consider different road standards that would bring down the public costs of development. No matter who has an interest in pursuing smart development strategies, this report will help address these concepts and help guide the reader to resources.

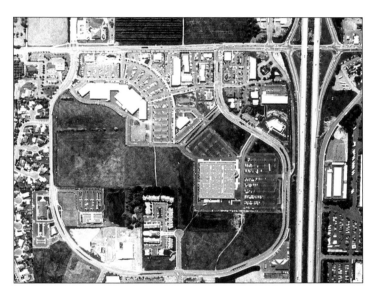

A typical, post-World War II development pattern. All the components of a town—city hall, library, church, college, post office, shopping center, apartments, and houses—are within walking distance, but are separated by vast, inhospitable parking lots, wide, nontransversable streets, or fragmented sidewalks.

The primary audience for this report is local planners, developers, and planning commissioners. Others who may find this document useful in seeking to encourage smart development in their communities include neighborhood and community activists, elected officials, and other citizens who ask why things cannot be done differently.

How to Initiate Change

Initiating smart development strategies in some communities may not require any changes in codes and standards; in others, it may require a few changes to allow for certain principles to be applied, and, in some cases, it may require more thorough, systemic change.

The decision to change local development codes in most cities and towns usually takes one of two forms: a comprehensive approach or a focused approach. In the first approach, a review of current development patterns and trends might show that smart development practices are not occurring. As a result, a thorough evaluation of procedures, codes, and standards would be performed. This review would scrutinize the obstacles and determine what might be done to encourage or allow use of these principles.

The second approach might evolve from a specific application for approval, a request for a code change to accommodate a development, or an effort undertaken by a jurisdiction to review a portion of its codes. As a

Change can start from a number of sources: a developer of a subdivision might suggest a new way to address land partitioning; a planner or planning commissioner might return from a conference where mixed uses were discussed and seek to apply the ideas to some of the community's neighborhood centers; or an elected official might want to consider different road standards that would bring down the public costs of development.

result of these actions, certain obstacles would become apparent. At that point, planners can make the decision to focus on specific obstacles or undertake a more general review.

Recognizing that there are many arrangements and combinations of codes in different communities, this report does not attempt to identify where barriers can be found in the regulatory structure. Instead, this report discusses specific obstacles and responses, leaving in local hands the determination of where changes might be needed. This report will help identify opportunities to use, encourage, or allow smart development principles. Ultimately, the decision of whether to use some or all of these principles will depend on how well they fit a community's goals and what the community's citizens and leaders want to achieve.

Chapter 1

The Principles of Smart Development

The following principles represent the most notable aspects of smart development. Together they describe an interconnected system of community building.

PRINCIPLE 1. EFFICIENT USE OF LAND RESOURCES

Smart development supports the preservation of land and natural resources. These benefits result from compact building forms, infill development, and moderation in street and parking standards. At the regional scale, cooperative growth management can encourage more compact development patterns, protecting farmland and open space from urban sprawl. At the local scale, compact building patterns preserve land for city and neighborhood parks as well as local woods and wetlands. Furthermore, compact development shortens trips, lessening dependence on the automobile, and therefore reducing levels of energy consumption and air pollution. Finally, a compact development pattern supports more cost-effective infrastructure than does low-density fringe development.

PRINCIPLE 2. FULL USE OF URBAN SERVICES

The same frugality of land development supports efficient use of public and private infrastructure. Smart development means creating neighborhoods where more people will use existing services like water lines and sewers, roads, emergency services, and schools. Inefficient land use, whether within or outside urban areas, places a financial strain on communities trying to provide for the construction and maintenance of infrastructure needs.

In Oregon, compact development patterns protect farmland from urban sprawl.

Building compactly does not mean that all areas must be densely developed. Rather, the goal is an average density for the area, at a level that makes full use of urban services. Averaging allows for areas to have a mix of low-, medium-, and high-density development. Mixing densities to encourage efficient use of services also means requiring a high level of building and siting compatibility, encouraging neighborhoods to have both character and privacy.

Careful street sizing and the accommodation of some parking on streets reduces impervious surfaces and efficiently uses urban services by saving on land acquisition, construction, and maintenance costs. In short, streets should be sized for their use: lower density areas that have little through traffic are best served by slower, narrower streets, while transportation corridors that move districtwide traffic need wider travelways.

PRINCIPLE 3. MIX OF USES

Locating stores, offices, residences, schools, and recreation spaces within walking distance of each other in compact neighborhoods with pedestrian-oriented streets promotes:

- independence of movement, especially for the young and the elderly who can conveniently walk, cycle, or ride transit;

- safety in commercial areas, through around-the-clock presence of people;

- reduction in auto use, especially for shorter trips;

- support for those who work at home, through nearby services and parks; and

- a variety of housing choices, so that the young and old, singles and families, and those of varying economic ability may find places to live.

Mixed-use examples include a corner store in a residential area, an apartment near or over a shop, and a lunch counter in an industrial zone. Most codes prohibit the colocation of any residential and commercial buildings. This prohibition is based on the functional and architectural incompatibility of the buildings. Using design standards, in tandem with mixed-use zoning, overcomes incompatibility. Additionally, limitations on commercial functions, such as hours of operation and delivery truck access, may be necessary. More fundamentally, to gain the full benefits of a mix of uses, buildings must be conveniently connected by streets and paths. Otherwise, people will still be inclined or required to use cars, even for the shortest trips.

Most codes prohibit the colocation of any residential and commercial buildings. This prohibition is based on the functional and architectural incompatibility of the buildings. Using design standards, in tandem with mixed-use zoning, overcomes incompatibility.

Building compactly means that neighborhoods make full use of existing urban services and can more easily afford amenities such as parks.

PRINCIPLE 4. TRANSPORTATION OPTIONS

Transportation must be safe, convenient, and interesting. These performance factors affect sidewalk and street design, placement of parking, and location of building fronts, doors, and windows. Well-designed bike lanes and sidewalks protect people from vehicle accidents. Orienting windows and doorways to the sidewalk increases awareness of street activity and the safety of the streetscape.

Convenience begins with a connected network of streets that provides alternative routes with reasonable walking distances between destinations. A properly designed network also promotes neighborhood safety by routing the heaviest traffic around neighborhoods, without sacrificing street connectivity. Field studies have shown that the level of aesthetic interest is a critical factor in choosing a walking route. People are unwilling to walk further than about 300 feet through a parking lot to reach a desired destination, yet they will walk at least three times that distance along a street of storefronts.

Providing compact, mixed-use development connected by safe, convenient, and interesting networks of streets and paths promotes:

- walking, cycling, and transit as viable, attractive alternatives to driving;

- less traffic congestion and air pollution;

- the convenience, density, and variety of uses necessary to support transit;

- a variety of alternative routes, thereby dispersing traffic congestion; and

- lower traffic speeds, making neighborhoods safer.

PRINCIPLE 5. DETAILED, HUMAN-SCALE DESIGN

Community acceptance of compact, mixed-use development requires compatibility between buildings to ensure privacy, safety, and visual coherency. Similar massing of buildings, orientation of buildings to the street, the presence of windows, doors, porches, and other architectural elements, and effective use of landscaping all contribute to successful compatibility between diverse building types.

Human-scale design is also critical to the success of streets and paths as preferred routes for pedestrians, cyclists, and motorists alike. In general, smart street design considers the role of pedestrians along with that of vehicular traffic, emphasizing the quality of the walking environment. For instance, parallel parking may be considered a hindrance to vehicle flow, but, for pedestrians and shop owners, on-street parking is a benefit because it reduces speeding traffic and protects the sidewalk.

Designing streets that are balanced for pedestrians, cyclists, and motorists promotes the development of community through the informal meeting of neighbors. Neighborhood safety is improved, since neighbors can more easily come to know one another and watch over each other's homes.

PRINCIPLE 6. IMPLEMENTATION

A community's ability to adopt smart development principles will, of necessity, require an examination of its development review process. What is a community looking for in this examination? Primarily, the review should focus on ways that the review process can be streamlined so that developers are encouraged to apply the principles. Frustrating, costly, and time-consuming delays due, in part, to inflexible standards,

Well-designed streets comfortably accommodate pedestrians, cyclists, and motorists.

Convenience begins with a connected network of streets that provides alternative routes with reasonable walking distances between destinations. A properly designed network also promotes neighborhood safety by routing the heaviest traffic around neighborhoods, without sacrificing street connectivity.

regulations, and processes will almost certainly doom any innovative approaches to development and design. Providing for flexibility and certainty in the application of standards, including provision for performance standards and administrative approval of "minor" variances, can help promote creative development that complies with the principles. Changes to the Planned Unit Development (PUD) process can also relieve some of the regulatory barriers for developers and lighten the administrative load for planners, as can adopting a flexible process for applying design review standards.

A community's ability to adopt smart development principles will, of necessity, require an examination of its development review process. Providing for flexibility and certainty in the application of standards, including provision for performance standards and administrative approval of "minor" variances, can help promote creative development that complies with the principles.

Porches are a human-scale design element that connects the public and private realms.

Chapter 2

Case Studies

The two case studies presented here offer examples of building projects that incorporate smart development principles in their designs. Fairview Village in Fairview, Oregon, was a large-parcel "greenfield" project, and Village Weistoria in Bend, Oregon, was a smaller, "infill" project.

FAIRVIEW VILLAGE, FAIRVIEW, OREGON
Developer: Holt and Haugh

Property Description:
- 137-acre undeveloped parcel within the City of Fairview

- Existing zoning: light manufacturing

Concept:
- A compact village that mixes uses either within the same area, on the same street, or in the same building.

- A connected street network with a hierarchy of designs ranging from 26 feet of pavement with parking on one side to 32 feet with parking on both sides. Parking allowed on all streets, except alleys (16-foot right-of-way).

Developer's Program

136 detached single-family units
50-60 accessory units
14 townhouses
110 rowhouses
26 duplexes
252 apartments
154,400 square feet of retail space
176,200 square feet of office space
40,000 square feet of public buildings
4.5 acres of natural open space
3.5 acres of formal parks
3.5 net units per acre

Fairview Village has a connected street network with a hierarchy of mixed-use designs.

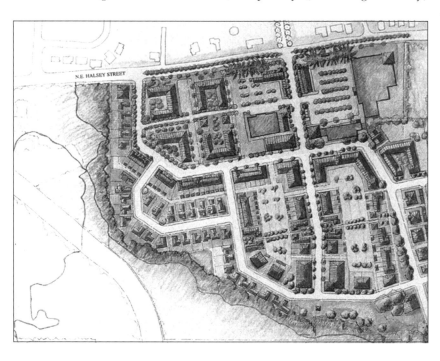

Because more than 20 variances would have been required to fulfill the plan, Holt and Haugh asked the city to amend its comprehensive plan to provide for a special plan district. The developer proposed that the company assume the burden of writing the new village zoning ordinance and that they fund an additional staff planner to handle the transition. To their credit, the city was open to the new zoning concepts and came to agreement with the developer.

- Multiple homeowner associations, design guidelines contained in the conditions, covenants, and restrictions.

- Uses include: retail, office, public uses (city hall, post office, parks), attached multifamily, detached single family, attached single family.

The 137-acre site within the city of Fairview was zoned light industrial when developers Holt and Haugh purchased it. There were no provisions within the city's zoning code for a mixed-use, mixed-density village. A rudimentary planned unit development provision allowed for transfer of density and flexibility of lot sizes, but the density and single-use limitations of the city's subdivision code still governed. The major code obstacles were:

- wide street standards based on conventional large suburban block sizes, with no provisions for curb-to-curb widths narrower than 36 feet;

- no provisions for alleys, mixing of uses, or accessory units;

- minimum front setbacks of 20 feet, with side setbacks of 15 feet, making small-lot development unfeasible; and

- minimum lot sizes that discouraged compact housing types.

Because more than 20 variances would have been required to fulfill the plan, Holt and Haugh asked the city to amend its comprehensive plan to provide for a special plan district. The developer proposed that the company assume the burden of writing the new village zoning ordinance and that they fund an additional staff planner to handle the transition. To their credit, the city was open to the new zoning concepts and came to agreement with the developer. The developer estimates to have incurred a 5 percent premium accredited to these extra efforts to remove obstacles to their unique, smart development.

The new "Fairview Village Special Plan District" features:

Basic architectural controls for the Fairview Village Special Plan District place garages behind the front of buildings.

- allowance for single-family accessory units, village townhomes, village apartments, village-mixed use (apartment or office over retail), village offices, public uses, and village commercial;

- a hierarchy of streets, including alleys, and curb-to-curb distances as little as 26 feet, with parking;

- basic architectural controls, including placement of garages—in most cases, behind the front of buildings;

- a riparian buffer overlay and conservation easement limit within a 50-foot horizontal distance from Fairview Creek that establishes the same distance as building setback;

- a policy for public parks to be developed by and reimbursed to the developer; and

- provisions for all stormwater to be captured on site.

VILLAGE WEISTORIA, BEND, OREGON

Developer: Village Development, Inc.

Property description:

- Seven-acre lot within the city of Bend (infill)

- Existing zoning: single-family residential (RS zone), 2.5 to 7.3 dwelling units per acre

- Buildings on site: single-family house, farm buildings

Concept:

- Compact village that provides modestly sized, attached and detached single-family housing within a walkable neighborhood, and includes parks and a community center.

- A connected street network with a hierarchy of designs ranging from 27-foot widths with parking on one side to 27-foot widths with parking on both sides and one lane of traffic. Parking to be allowed on all streets.

- Homeowner organization, design guidelines contained in the conditions, covenants, and restrictions.

- Desired uses included: retail buildings, offices, community buildings, detached and attached single-family residences, and accessory units.

The existing zoning for the property was a major obstacle to this plan. It allowed single-family residential only, with a minimum lot size of 6,000 square feet per unit. Also required were 32-foot-wide streets within a 60-foot right-of-way. No convenience commercial (e.g., corner store), light commercial (e.g., barber shop), or office use was permitted outright.

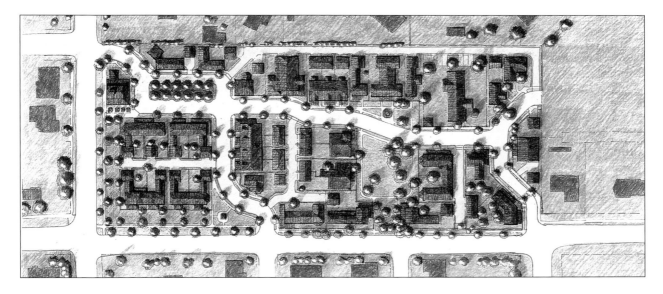

The Village Weistoria plan features a street network designed to connect with the surrounding neighborhood. The plan also preserved several old growth trees.

The existing zoning for the property was a major obstacle to this plan. It allowed single-family residential only, with a minimum lot size of 6,000 square feet per unit. Also required were 32-foot-wide streets within a 60-foot right-of-way. No convenience commercial (e.g., corner store), light commercial (e.g., barber shop), or office use was permitted outright.

In order to achieve the higher density and mix of housing types envisioned for the project, the developer avoided a zoning variance by using the planned unit development process. The developer also spent considerable time with the planning staff, the residents of the adjoining neighborhood, and the community explaining the project's goals and traditional neighbor-

Developer's program:

42 attached and detached single-family units
accessory units
2,600 square feet of public building
3.8 acres of public parks and roadways
14 net units per acre
Neighborhood "depot"—post office, meeting room, studio apartment

hood planning principles in general. He was able to show a majority of people the benefits of mixed use, mixed densities, connected streets, and moderated street design.

The primary obstacles to the project were:

- additional time spent on education and clarification in order to prevent future holdups;

- legal fees associated with a planned unit development; and

- subjective code standards that were left open to interpretation by city staff—certain guidelines were not clearly stated or understood.

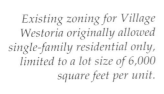

Existing zoning for Village Westoria originally allowed single-family residential only, limited to a lot size of 6,000 square feet per unit.

Chapter 3

Obstacles to Smart Development

Since regulatory and financing systems primarily serve single-use, conventional, and suburban development patterns and designs, builders often stick with this model, choosing what the existing system encourages rather than spending time and money trying to overcome barriers to smart development. One of the objectives of local leaders who want to encourage smart development should be to work with industry leaders to break down barriers and develop strategies to encourage more livable communities.

Though many older neighborhoods exemplify smart development, today's development industry is largely unfamiliar with the concept. Current regulatory and financial systems do not accommodate smart development, resulting in barriers that cause delays and increase costs. The cumulative effect of these barriers may frustrate developers who are trying to do smart development and may discourage others from pursuing projects in the future.

In deciding which projects to pursue, developers assess how various obstacles will hinder their ability to complete the project on time and affect the return on their investment. Since regulatory and financing systems primarily serve single-use, conventional, and suburban development patterns and designs, builders often stick with this model, choosing what the existing system encourages rather than spending time and money trying to overcome barriers to smart development. One of the objectives of local leaders who want to encourage smart development should be to work with industry leaders to break down barriers and develop strategies to encourage more livable communities.

An effort to bring together developers and community leaders took place in Oregon in 1996. On November 20, 1996, Livable Oregon, Inc., hosted Governor John Kitzaber's Symposium on Smart Development. The governor's symposium focused on barriers or obstacles that can make smart development projects more difficult or costly to build. These barriers can affect whether developers are able to successfully complete a project and may discourage them from pursuing smart development in the future. Based on interviews with developers from across Oregon, five common categories of barriers were identified and discussed at the symposium.

The first barrier is often local regulations. Poor or antiquated development codes (subdivision and zoning), lengthy approval processes, and excessive public facilities standards can discourage smart development. These codes, standards, and processes are based on conventional development patterns and normally do not have the flexibility to accommodate smart development, with its smaller lots, higher densities, mix of uses, narrower streets, and emphasis on providing a range of transportation options. In many cases, smart development projects require variances from development codes that can lead to costly delays.

Other identified barriers to smart development included:

- market conditions
- development and process costs
- financing
- community involvement

A full discussion of these other barriers is contained in Livable Oregon's survey on the conference, reprinted in Appendix A to this report.

Code obstacles to smart development are the focus of this report. These obstacles can interfere with smart development principles, often in different and sometimes subtle ways. Some obstacles are specific code requirements that may be excessive or prohibit smart development practices. Others fail to support smart development by their absence.

Overarching these impacts are inherent delays in the land-use approvals process. Process delays can include burdensome variance processes, discretionary design review, or excessive numbers of public hearings. Tracy Watson, the development process manager for the city of Austin, Texas, has said that, without a proposed "traditional neighborhood development" ordinance, the current code would require a smart development project to obtain 30 or more variances to gain approval. These kind of obstacles discourage developers from trying new approaches and encourage continuation of conventional development patterns.

The following is a brief discussion of code obstacles to smart development, grouped by the principles discussed in Chapter 1.

Obstacles to Efficient Land Use

Many smart development projects are infill development, often on parcels that may have an unusual shape or slope or other constraints that have caused developers to pass over the land in the past. Most codes rely on exact dimensioning of lot width, depth, and size. Most zones also have maximum density and minimum lot area requirements. These combine to produce a homogeneous development pattern that may not lend itself to the physical characteristics (i.e., slope, wetlands, riparian areas) of a particular parcel of land. Strictly applying these requirements to infill often results in fewer lots than if developers could cluster development or average dimension requirements within overall density maximums.

Smart development does not occur only on large sites as a single project but may involve infill development on small parcels or redevelopment of adjoining parcels with different ownership. Many codes do not have provisions to allow coordinated development of a multiparcel, multideveloper project.

Many development codes include outdated street design standards. These standards often require street widths too great for the traffic volumes they will carry, especially on local residential streets. When land is at a premium within an urban area, building excessively wide streets precludes the use of that land for housing or for amenities such as wider sidewalks or open space.

Finally, many codes include parking standards that require an excessive amount of land for parking. Standards are often based on models that assume every trip, no matter how short, will be made by car. For commercial areas, this results in large, separate parking lots for every building. This situation is especially problematic for smart development projects in neighborhood centers—designed for pedestrian friendliness and independence from the automobile. Furthermore, many codes do not have provisions that address shared parking arrangements or allow coordinated parking management plans.

Obstacles to Full Use of Urban Services

Smart development often means increasing the amount of housing in close proximity to other neighborhood services, such as shopping or transit. Higher-density development uses existing infrastructure more efficiently and can reduce the need for more capital improvements, such as sewer lines or roads.

Most zones also have maximum density and minimum lot area requirements. These combine to produce a homogeneous development pattern that may not lend itself to the physical characteristics (i.e., slope, wetlands, riparian areas) of a particular parcel of land.

Underbuilding (i.e., building significantly less than the maximum allowed density), is indicative of a common development practice: taking the path of least resistance. Many developers would prefer to build at the maximum density allowed but propose fewer units in an effort to head off community opposition. Many development codes do not include provisions to require minimum densities or maximum lot sizes. The underbuilding that results means an inefficient use of existing urban services, including parks, schools, and police and fire protection.

Development codes often do not have the flexibility to allow developers to fully use existing urban services by mixing housing types. Attached units (duplexes, rowhouses, or townhouses) can make full use of services by accommodating more units in less space, while providing for a range of housing types within a neighborhood. For example, many single-family zones require twice as much lot area for a duplex as a single-family home, providing no incentive to include duplexes in a development. Minimum lot size and side yard setback requirements can also bar the construction of attached units. Smart codes allow a variety of housing types, while setting appropriate standards to ensure design compatibility.

Allowing accessory units—small secondary units associated with single-family homes—can incrementally increase densities within a developed neighborhood while providing housing choices. These units, also known as "granny flats" or "in-law apartments," are often prohibited or must have a large enough lot to qualify for a second full-sized unit. Some communities allow accessory units but only if approved through a conditional use process, which can be a costly, confusing, and time-consuming process for a homeowner.

Obstacles to Mixed Use

The typical zoning code segregates and separates residential, commercial, and industrial uses. While smart development does not necessarily mean mixing industrial and residential uses, it does support mixing commercial and residential uses—prohibited in most codes except through a lengthy planned unit development process. Mixed use of this kind is not new: towns and neighborhood centers have historically included housing, often above shops and businesses, that can provide a steady source of customers for local businesses, especially after 5 p.m. By the same token, limited retail in a residential area allows people to more easily walk or bike to meet their daily needs, reducing reliance on the automobile.

Zoning codes also segregate different residential densities and housing types from one another. Rather than relying on design compatibility standards, communities often depend on oversized lots to buffer development, especially for attached units or multifamily apartment buildings. These practices also can lead to underbuilding: small buildings on large lots. For instance, one Oregon code requires a 100-foot building setback if a multifamily zone abuts a single-family zone, inevitably resulting in large parking lots straddling the zoning boundary. In another jurisdiction, the code requires the same lot area for a detached unit as for an attached one.

Obstacles to Transportation Options

Smart development results in land-use patterns that encourage walking, bicycling, and the use of mass transit as alternatives to automobile trips. Streets are the most prevalent public space in a community but are usually designed for the near-exclusive use of the automobile. Wide streets with large turning radii, built primarily to accommodate cars, can preclude features such as wider sidewalks or bicycle lanes that serve nondrivers.

Many developers would prefer to build at the maximum density allowed but propose fewer units in an effort to head off community opposition. Many development codes do not include provisions to require minimum densities or maximum lot sizes. The underbuilding that results means an inefficient use of existing urban services, including parks, schools, and police and fire protection.

Mixed-use development is not new: towns and neighborhood centers have historically included housing, often above shops and businesses, that can provide a steady source of customers for local businesses, especially after 5 p.m.

Streets are the most prevalent public space in a community but are usually designed for the near-exclusive use of the automobile. Wide streets with large turning radii, built primarily to accommodate cars, can preclude features such as wider sidewalks or bicycle lanes that serve nondrivers.

Also, in the past, development codes have rarely included limits on the length of cul-de-sacs or requirements for street connectivity that could eliminate pedestrian barriers and reduce out-of-direction travel.

Finally, many communities fail to recognize the opportunity to increase density within a quarter-mile of a transit stop, the area where people are most likely to walk to ride transit.

Obstacles to Detailed, Human-Scale Design

Opposition to new development sometimes comes from people opposed to growth, but it can also come from people with legitimate concerns about compatible design. Many development codes lack design guidelines or adequate transitions between land-use zones that mitigate compatibility problems. Others lack incentives for good design, such as density bonuses for including amenities like porches, bay windows, roof gables, or increased open space.

Many commercial zoning codes are written primarily to support the development of suburban shopping centers and malls. They encourage auto-oriented development with large setbacks from the street and expansive parking lots. While appropriate in some cases, these standards are often applied uniformly for all types of commercial development—a disaster for pedestrian-friendly neighborhood retail centers.

An Overarching Obstacle: The Development Review Process

A project of single-family detached houses—some with accessory units—and townhomes arranged around a small neighborhood commercial center would be prohibited outright in most codes. Gaining approval for such a project requires variances or a planned unit development approval, both of which can be so costly, time consuming, and burdensome that they deter most developers. Even communities with good design guidelines sabotage smart development proposals by involving them in a design review process that may be susceptible to subjective approvals. Integrating smart development principles into a code does not mandate them for all developments; instead, it creates the opportunity to employ them without a lengthy review process.

Opposition to new development sometimes comes from people opposed to growth, but it can also come from people with legitimate concerns about compatible design. Many development codes lack design guidelines or adequate transitions between land-use zones that mitigate compatibility problems. Others lack incentives for good design, such as density bonuses for including amenities like porches, bay windows, roof gables, or increased open space.

Chapter 4

Strategies and Solutions

This chapter outlines specific strategies that encourage smart development. All strategies are grouped according to the smart development principle from which they follow. Each strategy is accompanied by an obstacle and a solution to the obstacle. Table 1 on pages 20-21 provides a summarized version of the outline. Appendix B provides ordinance and plan language that might be useful in implementing the strategies described in this chapter.

1. EFFICIENT USE OF LAND RESOURCES

1.1

1.1 Strategy: Encourage Small-Lot Infill Development

Many residential neighborhoods, new and old, have been underbuilt because of circumstances of topography or history. Empty lots create gaps between neighbors, and buildable space at the end of the road sits overgrown and unused. Practicality and economic considerations push builders, today the same as 80 years ago, to place houses on the most standard, spacious, or accessible lots available. Buildable lots that are smaller, irregularly shaped, or affected by slopes are often passed over in the first wave of construction. The goal of using all valuable land, especially in areas where development has already taken place, provides a strong incentive to fill in these gaps in the fabric of a city or town.

1.1 Obstacle: Excessive Lot Area Dimensions

Small or irregularly shaped properties stay unbuilt in part because local jurisdictions either require overly large setbacks from neighboring property lines or forbid residential buildings on lots smaller than a certain number of square feet. If, for example, large side yard setbacks are required for a relatively narrow lot, the proposed house's width could be reduced to such a size that building it would no longer be feasible. Also, if the zoning code demands unnecessarily large minimum lot sizes for any construction to occur, building a house on an

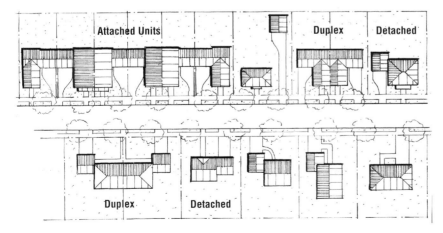

(Top) Smart development standards applied. Mix of lot sizes, minimum front setbacks, garages set back. (Bottom) Conventional development standards applied, uniform lot size, large front setbacks, garages in front of houses.

8,000-square-foot lot, spacious by most standards, may not be permitted if the code requires 10,000-square-foot minimums.

1.1 Solution: Revise Setback, Minimum Lot-Size Requirements

Revising setback and minimum lot-size requirements reduces barriers to infill development without adversely affecting existing neighborhoods. In fact, new buildings on smaller lots can add to the diversity of housing types in a neighborhood, enriching its character and improving its affordability. Reductions in the setback and lot-size requirements allow undersized lots to be filled with new housing and also increase the potential number of housing units in a zoning area. The new guidelines should modify existing standards: for instance, the city of Milwaukie, Oregon, reduced its minimum lot width in a type of single-family zone

Table 1. Principles, Strategies, Obstacles, and Solutions

STRATEGY	OBSTACLE	SOLUTION
1. Efficient Use of Land Resources		
1.1 Small-lot infill development	Excessive lot-area dimensions	Revise setback requirements; minimum lot sizes
1.2 Infill development on large lots	Inflexible subdivision and lot-area requirements	Average lot size for whole development, allow flexibility to preserve natural features
1.3 Coordinated development	Coordinated development not addressed	Specific development plans; master plans
1.4 Better use of deep lots	Excessive frontage and multiple access requirements	Midblock lanes; interior block cluster development; flag lots
1.5 Less land for streets	Excessive street design standards	Adopt "skinny" street standards
1.6 More efficient use of parking areas	Excessive parking requirements	Reduce minimum parking ratios; set parking ratio maximums; acknowledge on-street parking; encourage shared parking
2. Full Use of Urban Services		
2.1 Achieving planned densities	Underbuilding; no support for density goals	Minimum density standards
2.2 Attached units	Lot sizes not in proportion to unit sizes	Reduce lot-size requirements; allow single-family attached in all residential zones
2.3 Attached units	Lot-area dimension requirements (excessive side setbacks)	Revise setback requirements
2.4 Accessory units	Excessive minimum unit size; density maximums too low	Allow accessory units
3. Mixed Use		
3.1 Mixed-use buildings	Single-use zoning; separation of uses	Allow home occupations and live/work units; density bonus for mixed-use commercial/residential buildings
3.2 Mixed-use neighborhoods	Single-use zoning; separation of uses	Limited commercial in residential zones; allow multifamily residential in commercial zones; limited retail in industrial zones
3.3 Healthy commercial districts	Separation of uses; proximity	Community shopping centers with street connectivity; main street districts

from 70 feet to 50 feet and reduced minimum lot size in a multifamily district from 5,000 to 3,000 square feet.

1.2

1.2 Strategy: Encourage Infill Development on Large Lots

For larger parcels of land or for new subdivisions, efficient use of land calls for a neighborhood where every square foot is well designed and used to the utmost. Because of economies of scale, developers normally favor real estate where they can build a larger number of houses at one time. These parcels are ideal locations for innovation that results in healthy, smartly developed neighborhoods, providing benefits and choices to residents.

Table 1. Continued

STRATEGY	OBSTACLE	SOLUTION
4. Transportation Options		
4.1 Multimodal streets	Street design standards overemphasize autos	Revise street standards; promote "skinny" streets
4.2 Transit, bike, and pedestrian connectivity	Physical barriers or out-of-direction travel	Cul-de-sac and block-length maximums; internal connectivity standards; sidewalk requirements
4.3 Transit-supportive development	Transit-supportive development not addressed	Mandate transit-oriented development along transit corridor
5. Detailed, Human-Scale Design		
5.1 Compatibly designed buildings	Too abrupt transitions between zones	Density transitioning; midblock zoning district lines; building height limits
5.2 Compatibly designed buildings	No design guidelines for new buildings	Incorporate compatibility guidelines for new infill construction
5.3 Pedestrian-friendly streetscapes (commercial)	Street standards emphasize cars; design discourages walking	Building orientation; parking lot placement; allow shared access; 50%/80% frontage rule; etc.
5.4 Pedestrian-friendly streetscapes (residential)	Street standards emphasize cars; design discourages walking	Require sidewalks; limit setbacks; garage placement; lighting; utility placement; etc.
5.5 Quality architectural design	No incentive to provide amenities	Density bonuses for amenities
6. Implementation		
6.1 Examining the development review process	Onerous procedures for variances, conditional uses	Allow administrative approval for minor adjustments
6.2 Examining the Planned Unit Development (PUD) process	Onerous PUD requirements	Improved PUD regulations
6.3 Flexibility in the design review process	Discretionary design review process; vague standards	Dual-track design review process

1.2 Obstacle: Inflexible Subdivision and Lot-Area Requirements

Though developers generally prefer sites where they can build many houses at once, overly restrictive, complex zoning codes or subdivision requirements can either create bland, cookie-cutter developments where every house is nearly the same or discourage construction altogether. Strict lot-area requirements result in predictable and relatively homogenous building types and do not encourage builders to avoid environmentally sensitive areas. In addition, uniform lot requirements tend to oversize lots for development with attached units or multifamily developments. In at least one Oregon city, the code requires the same area per unit for a individual house as for an attached one (i.e., 5,000 square feet for a single-family home and 10,000 square feet for a duplex). This eliminates the land savings that draws builders to consider attached units in the first place.

1.2 Solution: Average Lot Size for Whole Development; Encourage Flexibility to Preserve Natural Amenities

The ability to vary lot dimensions gives builders the necessary flexibility to vary housing type, providing greater market choice. Most codes rely on exact dimensioning of width, depth, and area to address neighborhood compatibility. A smarter route for promoting diverse housing types in a new development is to control what really matters: the average overall sizes of the lots. This enables builders to build according to site conditions, and to mix together single-family and multifamily units. For compatibility's sake, subdivision and zoning codes should establish limits on the range of possibilities. For instance, codes could allow single-family homes to mix with duplexes but not to abut directly with large apartment buildings. A smart development zoning code achieves a dual goal: it allows flexibility for the developer to provide a variety of housing types while ensuring the public that buildings will be compatible with each other and with adjoining neighborhoods.

Strict lot-area requirements result in predictable and relatively homogenous building types and do not encourage builders to avoid environmentally sensitive areas. In addition, uniform lot requirements tend to oversize lots for development with attached units or multifamily developments.

A smart development zoning code achieves a dual goal: it allows flexibility for the developer to provide a variety of housing types while ensuring the public that buildings will be compatible with each other and with adjoining neighborhoods.

This master plan pinpoints the location of streets, building lots, parks, and open space.

1.3

1.3 Strategy: Coordinated Development

Large undeveloped areas are often comprised of multiple ownership. Different goals between property owners or simply a lack of communication can unnecessarily fragment new development. Establishing an overall specific or refinement plan in advance can ensure the area is built in a coherent fashion. These plans provide a framework for locating smart development features, such as a connected network of streets, neighborhood parks, and mixed uses and densities. Specific plans provide certainty for all parties: the city, developers, and the neighbors. Since the overall plan has already passed city and neighborhood review, developers know what standards they must follow and spend much less time getting approval for particular elements of site design and construction. In turn, the plan provides certainty for the city and the neighbors as to the quality of the development.

1.3 Obstacle: Coordinated Development Not Addressed

A primary problem of growing cities and towns is piecemeal, uncoordinated development. Undeveloped land is often parceled into many separate holdings, each with a variety of sizes and configurations. If these parcels develop independently, it is very difficult to coordinate features (e.g., an overall network of connected streets or neighborhood parks). Standard subdivision requirements that prescribe open space requirements and street connections may not go far enough, resulting in uncoordinated, patchwork development, rather than a coherent neighborhood.

1.3 Solution: Specific Development Plans

In order to initiate a specific plan, the comprehensive plan must first be amended to allow for specific, geographically defined planning areas. Nearby neighbors and landowners within the planning area should be involved in the planning process. Specific plans regulate the location of streets, parks, and open space, prescribe allowed uses, and can control building placement and design. Street and public facility location can be contentious issues for landowners. Also, planning streets that guarantee connectivity and that allow individual owners to develop independently can occasionally be difficult, requiring two or more owners to develop together. For example, to maintain connectivity between landholdings, streets should either connect to those of the neighboring parcel or "stub-out" to allow for future connections.

Establishing an overall specific or refinement plan in advance can ensure the area is built in a coherent fashion. These plans provide a framework for locating smart development features, such as a connected network of streets, neighborhood parks, and mixed uses and densities. Specific plans provide certainty for all parties: the city, developers, and the neighbors.

1.4

1.4 Strategy: Better Use of Deep Lots

In some areas, lots in existing neighborhoods may have standard widths but be unusually deep compared to other lots in the area. Essentially unused space at the back of a lot provides an ideal place for infill development, especially since this kind of growth brings a relatively small impact to an existing neighborhood. When correctly controlled, adding residential units on deep lots can bring a greater choice of housing types to a neighborhood and make more efficient use of land.

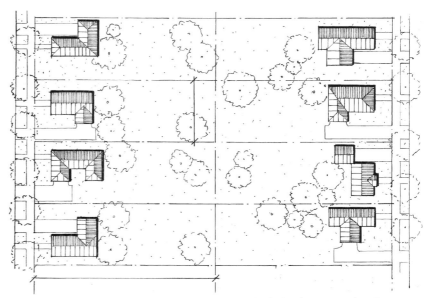

Existing houses on deep lots. See the illustration on page 24 for an example of smart development of these lots.

1.4 Obstacle: Excessive Frontage and Multiple Access Requirements

Unfortunately, many codes have requirements that effectively make developing deep lots impossible. Requiring a minimum amount of street frontage for each residential unit, for example, keeps the frontage-less land at the back of a deep lot empty. In addition, access requirements sometimes mandate that each unit has its own driveway, meaning that adding a unit would require adding a second driveway onto the street, resulting in wasteful and unsightly paving taking up too much of the lot's street frontage and creating unsafe traffic conditions.

1.4 Solution: Midblock Lanes; Interior-Block Cluster Developments; Flag Lots

For areas that have consistently extra deep blocks, say of 300 feet or greater, a series of interconnected midblock lanes could be provided to serve the new residences. Through a specific or refinement plan, a 10-foot easement on each side of the rear lot line could allow for a 20-foot-wide lane to connect the midblock units to the existing street system.

Another solution to tap this land resource is an interior block cluster development, a design that deals with an irregularly shaped parcel of land

Existing Houses **New Houses**

Shared Rear Lane

Shared Side Drive

Midblock infill development using new network of interconnected lanes. See the illustration on page 23 for the original configuration of these lots.

surrounded by existing residences. A single, connecting lane can extend from one side of the block to the other, with residences clustering around the center of the block. Each building would have street access via the new lane, without the overwhelming effect of more driveways onto the main neighborhood street. A 42-unit infill project in northeast Portland, Oregon, will include a midblock lane, making the most of the available land.

Lastly, development codes can be revised to allow for "flag lot" residences at the back of very deep lots, without adding lanes, by simply permitting shared driveways and changing street frontage requirements. Since this solution does not increase connectivity, it should be the last choice among the available infill options.

1.5

1.5 Strategy: Less Land for Streets

> When land is at a premium, building neighborhoods with excessively wide streets precludes using that land for more productive and profitable uses. Each square foot of land paved over for the purpose of automobile travel is a square foot made unavailable for a sidewalk, a yard, floor space in a house or store, or open space.

When land is at a premium, building neighborhoods with excessively wide streets precludes using that land for more productive and profitable uses. Each square foot of land paved over for the purpose of automobile travel is a square foot made unavailable for a sidewalk, a yard, floor space in a house or store, or open space. Smart development demands that wasted space be captured, and one of the easiest places to find that wasted land is in streets.

1.5 Obstacle: Excessive Street Design Standards

Often, street standards for residential neighborhoods are based on outdated assumptions of possible traffic volumes or the needs of atypically large vehicles. Street widths often are much greater than is needed for ordinary use, not only wasting land but encouraging speeding cars and cut-through traffic. Furthermore, since local governments often have responsibility for constructing and maintaining streets, greater-than-necessary standards drive up municipal costs. Many streets are designed primarily for conditions that may occur only infrequently or possibly not at all on that street, making it an inappropriate environment for the people who use it on a daily basis.

1.5 Solution: Street Standards Appropriate to Street Function; Adopt "Skinny" Street Standards

Guidelines from the Institute of Transportation Engineers state that a "street should be no wider than the minimum width needed to accommodate the typical and usual vehicular mix that the street will serve." This common sense strategy means that residential streets should be built at a variety of widths, depending on their function and hierarchy in the street system. Moreover, research has shown the necessary width of a street can be even narrower than conventional wisdom would suggest. Portland, Oregon, discovered that, after crossing a certain threshold, street widths can be dramatically narrowed with no loss of functional performance. Through field testing, the city also discovered that the space needed for emergency vehicles was less than previously thought. This research resulted in the adoption of "skinny" street standards that call for streets that use land sensibly, require less money to build, and offer a friendlier environment to pedestrians and residents.

In a Portland, Oregon, field test, a fire truck passes on a 20-foot-wide street.

1.6

1.6 Strategy: More Efficient Use of Parking

Space required for the storage of automobiles is a major drain on precious land resources. Especially as cities and towns grow, making land more valuable, property previously devoted to parking becomes attractive for more productive uses. The amount of parking required by a project, either by the code or by the market, is the biggest determining factor for a building's "footprint" on the site and the number of square feet in the finished structure. A single parking space can require up to 300 square feet of land, the same amount of floor space in a small studio apartment. Smart development encourages builders and planners to find ways to reduce the need for parking, to make the most of space devoted to parking, and to minimize the impact of parking on neighborhoods.

1.6 Obstacle: Excessive Parking Requirements

Code requirements, both residential and commercial, usually demand that a significant amount of land be given over for automobile storage. For residential developments, parking ratios are set as high as two or more off-street parking spaces for every unit, regardless of unit size. Requirements for parking in commercial developments are often set at what can be expected at the busiest time of the year, creating paved over, unused land 360 days out of the year. Excessive minimum parking requirements, but no maximum requirements, or limits, result in an inefficient use of land resources.

Excessive minimum parking requirements, but no maximum requirements, or limits, result in an inefficient use of land resources.

1.6 Solutions: Reduce Minimum Parking Ratios; Establish Parking Ratio Maximums; Allow On-Street Parking; Encourage Shared Parking

Reducing minimum parking ratios allows builders of commercial structures the opportunity to do more with the recaptured land, such as landscaping or placing more square footage within the new building. Reducing the minimum parking ratios can create tremendous savings for the property owner, in both land and development costs. For example, constructing a 100,000-square-foot building with a parking ratio of three spaces per 1,000 square feet of building, rather than four spaces per 1,000, saves almost an acre of usable land. In many commercial areas today, that acre could be worth $800,000.

In growing areas, setting a parking ratio maximum, or ceiling, helps hold down the amount of land given over for automobile storage. An upper limit forces builders to build only as much parking on the site as they really need and encourages closer study of parking supply and demand. More land-efficient parking methods—public shared lots, carpool spaces, structures—could be exempt from the parking ceiling requirement.

Many commercial areas, recognizing the importance of parking, have benefited from a carefully thought out parking management plan. A coordinated effort between businesses can reduce the need for unnecessary parking and open up more land for other uses. Such a plan optimizes the use of existing lots, encourages shared parking, and provides incentives to use modes other than the car. Businesses and planners should also acknowledge on-street parking as a valuable resource, primarily for its low-impact ability to store customers' cars, and also as a tool that slows traffic and provides a buffer for pedestrians. Codes can be modified to count on-street parking toward the minimum ratio required.

Parking standards should be modified to allow cooperation between businesses. For example, a bank and a restaurant could take advantage of different peak demand times by sharing a common lot or at least permitting access between lots.

> Constructing a 100,000-square-foot building with a parking ratio of three spaces per 1,000 square feet of building, rather than four spaces per 1,000, saves almost an acre of usable land. In many commercial areas today, that acre could be worth $800,000.

Diagonal parking on this main sreet reduces the need for parking lots, a savings for the whole community.

Residential areas have also found innovative ways to manage parking. For instance, the manager of Ankeny Woods, a transit-oriented, multifamily development in east Portland, Oregon, offers a cash "parking space rebate" to residents who agree not to own a car. If enough residents take advantage of the program, the project has been designed so that some of the land currently dedicated to car storage can be converted into a basketball court or playground for children who live in the complex. If enough programs like this succeed, future projects can plan more housing units on land that had previously been required for parking.

> A coordinated effort between businesses can reduce the need for unnecessary parking and open up more land for other uses. Such a plan optimizes the use of existing lots, encourages shared parking, and provides incentives to use modes other than the car.

2. FULL USE OF URBAN SERVICES

2.1

2.1 Strategy: Achieving Planned Densities
Each new home in a city or town carries an associated cost of supporting public infrastructure—roads and sidewalks to get to it, sewer lines to carry waste away from it, and firefighters to keep it from burning down, to name a few. Smart development encourages people to live where these expensive public services

already exist, rather than pushing at the edges of the urban area and creating new demand. Because of economies of scale, more residences within a prescribed area result in lower public infrastructure costs per unit. People living closer together can share the same sewer lines, roads, and other infrastructure, making better use of existing urban services.

2.1 Obstacle: Underbuilding, No Support for Density Goals

Because of a number of barriers, including regulatory or community opposition, neighborhoods and builders lose opportunities to build out fully, or they spread development out over a larger space than is necessary. Underbuilt existing neighborhoods can be dotted with empty lots, and new development may be underbuilt by creating large-lot development at very low densities. Such development (or lack thereof) makes poorer use of urban services than denser development for which facilities have been planned, built, and financed. Since infrastructure costs, to some extent, are spread out throughout the whole community, other neighborhoods end up partially subsidizing the infrastructure costs for underbuilt areas.

Despite the cost-efficiency for both local municipalities and for developers, denser development receives little support for several reasons. Codes may allow lower densities than are ideal, or communities may outright oppose the idea of higher densities. Ironically, many places where new residences could be accommodated with the lowest cost to public infrastructure are the same places where neighbors often strenuously oppose infill development. In fact, many of these neighborhoods have density "deficits"; that is, not enough people live there to adequately support a full array of urban services, such as a corner store, a full-time police officer, or a school. As a result, residents of low-density areas must leave their neighborhoods to satisfy many of their everyday needs.

2.1 Solution: Minimum Density Standards

Many codes only set a maximum density level to provide a safeguard against overbuilding, but do not prevent developers from underusing property. Minimum standards for density prevent building patterns that are expensive to serve with public infrastructure.

In setting a new goal for a minimum density for an area, planners should consider the surrounding densities but not let this limit their possibilities. In Clackamas County, Oregon, for example, developers have complained that, although they would like to build higher density projects in some cases, ordinances do not allow more intense development than the adjoining, 1970s era, low-density neighborhoods. Density minimums in Oregon are not new. In 1985, Springfield, Oregon, adopted minimum density zoning in medium- and high-density residential areas to make their zoning consistent with their comprehensive plan. Nevertheless, setting a standard presents a challenge: one that is too low may result in undesirably sparse development, and one that is too high may deter builders from doing a project at all. Local planners and public officials should work with developers to set a number that is within the range of market demand.

2.2 _____

2.2 Strategy: Attached Units

Attached units, whether duplexes, rowhouses, or townhouses, make full use of urban services by accommodating more residents in less space than detached units, while still allowing neighborhood compatibility. The developer gains savings in land and construction costs, and the public benefits from a more efficient use of sewer lines, police patrols, and the like.

The first step to encouraging denser development, and the public savings that follow from it, is to set—or set higher—minimum density standards. . . . Setting a standard presents a challenge: one that is too low may result in undesirably sparse development, and one that is too high may deter builders from doing a project at all. Local planners and public officials should work with developers to set a number that is within the range of market demand.

A new duplex fits comfortably with its older, single, detached neighbors. Similar massing and de-emphasizing garage doors aids building compatibility.

In some communities' codes, even duplexes are classified as multifamily housing, and as such, forbidden in single-family zones. This shortsighted approach disregards the benefits that well-designed attached housing can bring to a neighborhood.

Attached units increase the savings on infrastructure even more than closely spaced, detached units since attached housing can share resources like a single sewer connection or driveway. As infill in neighborhoods of predominantly single-family detached homes, duplexes and townhouses can add variety to the housing types without substantially changing neighborhood character.

2.2 Obstacle: Lot Sizes Not in Proportion to Unit Size; Attached Units Not Allowed

Code requirements sometimes set out strict standards for the minimum lot size per unit. This view assumes that all houses in a neighborhood will be detached single-family homes, creating a major roadblock for the building of attached units. If each residence is required to sit on its own fixed-size plot of land, builders have no incentive to use less space or to create more units with attached housing.

In some communities' codes, even duplexes are classified as multifamily housing, and as such, forbidden in single-family zones. This shortsighted approach disregards the benefits that well-designed attached housing can bring to a neighborhood.

2.2 Solution: Reduce Minimum Required Lot Size; Allow Single-Family Attached in Residential Zones

Smaller lots overall and more flexible requirements for attached housing in particular will help encourage denser development. A smaller minimum lot size allows the maximum number of units to be built, or at least gives greater choice to builders in making the decision.

Furthermore, codes could be modified to allow single-family attached housing in all residential zones. Corner lots are especially appropriate locations for attached housing within a neighborhood of mostly detached houses. If carefully designed, the impact of attached housing on existing neighborhoods is small and could be permitted outright, without triggering any kind of variance or review process.

2.3

2.3 Strategy: Attached Units

See the benefits of attached units discussed the previous section.

2.3 Obstacle: Lot-Area Dimensions (excessive side yard requirements)

Another barrier to attached housing is building codes that require side setbacks for all buildings, making the attachment of two units impossible. As a roundabout way of addressing neighborhood compatibility, codes usually rely on exact dimensioning of lot width, depth, and area. This allows only one type of housing to be feasible. For infill, attached units are especially attractive on unusual or irregular lots that are slightly larger than the average, but less than two full lots. If all units are required to have 10-foot setbacks from each other and from adjoining property lines, a builder would have to give up on the idea of a slightly wider duplex and instead construct a single house, effectively underbuilding the lot. Overly large setbacks can overwhelm an already tight site plan.

2.3 Solution: Revise Setback Requirements

Setback requirements, particularly side setback requirements, should be revised so as not to implicitly forbid attached housing. Such revisions offer developers a wider range of choices when deciding what kind of housing to build on a site and make the prospect of attached housing more attractive. In addition, smaller lot sizes eliminate the owner's need to maintain a part of a lot for which there is relatively little use and could, in some circumstances, increase privacy.

Ultimately, code requirements for setbacks should be proportional to the lot size and the proposed building. Excessive setbacks encourage less living space devoted to people and more space devoted to grass and asphalt.

2.4

2.4 Strategy: Accessory Units

An accessory unit is a small, secondary unit on a single-family lot, usually the size of a studio apartment. The additional unit could be above a garage or in a portion of an existing house. These spaces allow for a different housing choice within a typically homogenous neighborhood. An accessory unit can give the homeowner a place for a family member, such as an elderly parent, to live independently while maintaining a connection to the household. It also could be rented out as a studio apartment, the income dedicated to paying the mortgage of the primary household. A high level and quality of management is ensured by the fact that homeowners themselves oversee the accessory units. While providing benefits to individual homeowners, mixing this kind of less expensive housing into established neighborhoods also benefits the whole area by reducing the demand for large apartment projects and providing greater choice.

From the Irvington neighborhood in Portland to Pacific Terrace in Klamath Falls, accessory units have existed compatibly in single-family and mixed-use neighborhoods in Oregon for many years, adding diversity to established areas. Even in exclusive residential communities such as Del Mar, California, accessory units in single-family neighborhoods have almost become the norm rather than the exception.

This accessory unit over a garage is limited in size and is architecturally compatible.

> Setback requirements, particularly side setback requirements, should be revised so as not to implicitly forbid attached housing. Such revisions offer developers a wider range of choices when deciding what kind of housing to build on a site and make the prospect of attached housing more attractive. . . . Ultimately, code requirements for setbacks should be proportional to the lot size and the proposed building.

2.4 Obstacle: Excessive Minimum Unit Size; Density Maximums Too Low

Most codes either forbid accessory units outright or make them a conditional use, a difficult barrier to overcome. If accessory units are not addressed specifically in the code, often other regulations effectively prevent them, such as minimum unit size or density maximums. If a single-family zone requires all residences to be have at least 1,500 square feet of floor space, creating a 500-square-foot accessory unit is out of the question. If the maximum neighborhood density is so low that no more units of any kind are permitted, a homeowner who would like to build an addition to his house to accommodate a student or a relative would not have that option.

2.4 Solution: Revise Requirements for Unit Size; Revise Densities to Allow Accessory Units

Changing the regulatory requirements that either explicitly or effectively bar accessory units is the first step to encouraging their construction. The most obvious trouble spots in the code are normally connected to minimum unit size, maximum allowable densities, setbacks, and access requirements. Additionally, compatibility requirements should be added to ensure an easy fit with the neighborhood. The keys to compatible development of the units include: owner occupation of the primary unit, unit sizes of around 500 square feet, access and/or parking provisions, and careful window placement to aid privacy.

The most obvious trouble spots in a code (as regards accessory units) are normally connected to minimum unit size, maximum allowable densities, setbacks, and access requirements. Additionally, compatibility requirements should be added to ensure an easy fit with the neighborhood.

3. MIXED USE

3.1

3.1 Strategy: Mixed-Use Buildings

Mixing uses within buildings—a repair shop with an apartment above, or an accountant who both lives and works in his home—combines more activities together in the same area and reduces the need for people to drive. Integrating housing with other uses also increases neighborhood safety by maintaining activity in residential areas during the day and in commercial centers after 5 p.m. A small business, such as a cafe or a corner store, can add to the quality and convenience of a residential neighborhood.

3.1 Obstacle: Single-Use Zoning; Separation of Uses

Zoning was initially used to separate uses, such as preventing the mixing of textile factories or hog farms with residences. Over time, zoning laws expanded the number of distinctions between uses, resulting in more and more segregation until virtually all types of uses were separated from one another. Most residential areas do not allow stores, offices, or even other kinds of residences within their zoning districts.

Operating a small business on the same site as one's residence eliminates a daily commute, allows parents to be home more often, and adds to the safety of the neighborhood.

3.1 Solution: Flexibility in Residential Zoning; Density Bonus for Mixed-Use Commercial/Residential Buildings; Allow Home Occupations

Allowing mixed-use buildings where they are currently prohibited, and using density bonuses to encourage the construction of new mixed-use buildings are two methods that promote mixed use. For builders or renovators interested in smart development, a mixed-use zone offers some exciting opportunities.

A "live-work" unit, a limited business operating on the first floor of a primary residence, is a good way to integrate uses into a homogenous neighborhood. The ability of someone to operate a small business on the same site as one's residence can be a benefit to the person and the neighborhood in many ways: it eliminates a daily commute; it allows parents to be home more often; it adds to the safety of the neighborhood by having someone home during the day; it can buoy up a business that could not afford rent in a commercial district; and, in more concentrated areas, it can activate neighborhood retail locations. In fact, live-work units were the beginning of many great shopping streets, including Portland's Northwest 23rd Avenue, and Newbury Street in Boston, Massachusetts. These residential streets incubated small, home-based operations that eventually matured into viable, stand-alone businesses.

For live-work units to thrive, certain guidelines and controls should be applied: a small or zero front-yard setback, an area of operation no larger than around 1,250 square feet, a main entrance that faces the primary street, a limited number of employees, and no more than four off-street parking spaces for the business and two for the residence.

A cafe live/work unit with the main entrance facing the street and parking placed behind.

3.2

3.2 Strategy: Mixed-Use Neighborhoods

Smart development combines many activities in the same area, reversing the pattern of single-purpose neighborhoods. Commercial, retail, education, recreation, and residential uses commingle and benefit from each other's energy. By bringing different services closer to housing, mixed-use neighborhoods also offer the option of walking or biking to school, shopping, or work, thereby reducing the amount of time people spend driving.

3.2 Obstacle: Single-Use Zoning; Separation of Uses

Zoning, originally a tool to keep noxious uses separate from residential areas, gradually evolved into a system that keeps every aspect of daily life separate from every other. Work, shopping, school, and home are all divided from one another. Under the strict mandate of many residential zoning codes, a corner store is categorized as an unacceptable incursion into the neighborhood, as noxious and damaging as an oil refinery. Likewise, people are forbidden from living in commercial areas, leaving downtown or main street districts desolate after regular work hours.

This corner store fits in the neighborhood by maintaining a residential scale and limiting its operations.

3.2 Solution: Limited Commercial in Residential Zones; Multifamily Residential Allowed in Commercial Zones; Limited Retail Allowed in Industrial Zones

Several basic land-use elements are necessary to support smart development, all of them dealing with the mixing of uses.

In residential areas, allowing limited retail services provides access to daily needs and potential for an informal social center or gathering place. In some older neighborhoods, neighborhood retail centers survive and allow nearby residents to more easily walk or bike to pick up a quart of milk, bring children to day care, or drop off dry cleaning. In order for such retail services to thrive and to remain compatible with neighborhood character, the following guidelines should be followed: commercial use limited to the ground floor; a building footprint no larger than 2,500 square feet; on-street parking required in front of the building; the main entrance facing the primary street; off-street parking limited to five spaces for the commercial use; limited hours of operation (e.g., to between 7 a.m. and 10 p.m.); no drive-through businesses; and, possibly, prohibitions on the sale of carry-out alcoholic beverages.

Conversely, mixing certain types of housing into commercial zones can inject life into business districts. Multifamily housing in commercial zones should be allowed as a way for residents to reduce car travel for all daily activities, as well as a prime location for senior housing. Permitting multifamily buildings in a commercial zone allows developers to respond to several markets simultaneously and broadens their ability to respond to changing market forces. For instance, a developer of a new Safeway supermarket in the Rose City Park neighborhood of Portland, Oregon, used a corner of the large lot to build senior housing that has responded well to the market. However, single-family, detached housing should not be allowed in commercial zones, since such an influx of housing would effectively "downzone" the area and harm the commercial vitality of the business center; new housing in commercial areas should be limited to multifamily dwellings.

Industrial zones also can permit limited commercial activity, under certain circumstances. As employment centers, industrial areas teem with workers during the day, people who would benefit from amenities like a small-scale store, lunch counter, or bank. Even small motels for visiting business people may be acceptable. Such businesses can satisfy some of the workers' needs without forcing them to drive several miles to the nearest commercial zone just to buy a sandwich.

3.3

3.3 Strategy: Healthy Commercial Districts

Neighborhood commercial districts, by mixing uses within general areas, contribute to the livelihood of a community and reduce the need for long, frequent automobile trips. Healthy small-scale commercial districts give a unique identity and character to the surrounding area, creating a places of local interest and pride where people can feel comfortable shopping or strolling.

3.3 Obstacle: Separation of Uses; Proximity

A great deal of new postwar development has divided uses so dramatically that there is no space for neighborhood commercial areas between the large tracts of single-family houses. Some existing neighborhood commercial districts have lost customers as a result of the boom in large shopping malls and "big box" retailers, which cater exclusively to people arriving by automobile. Development codes actively promote the siting

---

In residential areas, allowing limited retail services provides access to daily needs and potential for an informal social center or gathering place. . . . Conversely, mixing certain types of housing into commercial zones can inject life into business districts.

Industrial zones also can permit limited commercial activity, under certain circumstances. As employment centers, industrial areas teem with workers during the day, people who would benefit from amenities like a small-scale store, lunch counter, or bank. Even small motels for visiting business people may be acceptable.

of big chain stores near highways since they are located in commercial zones, but at the same time they often discourage new small businesses placed closer to consumers, within existing neighborhood commercial districts.

3.3 Solution: Community Shopping Centers; Main Street Districts

Adjusting standards to allow for commercial activity to exist and thrive closer to the source of its customers is smart both for merchants and for municipalities. Building on successful elements of existing community shopping centers and main street districts helps keep mixed-use areas viable; supporting new business development in areas that are potentially mixed use has the same effect. By changing codes that permit new commercial development only in single-use commercial zones, planners open the door for new development in older commercial districts, which are normally closer to residential neighborhoods. If new commercial development chooses a site next to a residential area, planners should take full advantage of their proximity and should mandate connectivity between the two areas.

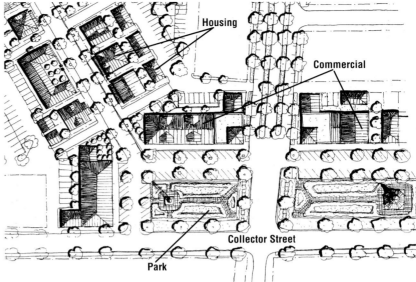

Traffic on the abutting collector streets supports a neighborhood commerical center, while pedestrian-friendly routes are available for residents of the attached neighborhood.

4. TRANSPORTATION OPTIONS

4.1

4.1 Strategy: Multimodal Streets

Smart development depends on people having a range of transportation options to get where they need to go, and, just as importantly, infrastructure on which to carry out these options. Streets are the most prevalent of public spaces, touching virtually every parcel of private land. If people choose to walk or bike on neighborhood streets, they should feel welcome and safe, just as much as people who choose to drive. Streets designed with many different users in mind will encourage nonmotorist travel, bettering the health of the community and making it more livable. Without a comfortable and safe street environment for all users, people will continue to rely on the car for every trip to and from the home, making many of the other smart development objectives difficult to achieve.

Streets are the most prevalent of public spaces, touching virtually every parcel of private land. If people choose to walk or bike on neighborhood streets, they should feel welcome and safe, just as much as people who choose to drive. Without a comfortable and safe street environment for all users, people will continue to rely on the car for every trip to and from the home, making many of the other smart development objectives difficult to achieve.

4.1 Obstacle: Streets Designed Exclusively for Cars

Street planners have traditionally followed standards that focus too narrowly on one category of user—the driver—at the expense of other users: pedestrians and cyclists. The greater the emphasis on a narrow group of users for a particular street, the less appealing it will be for those who want to choose other ways of travel. The true challenge in making streets more genuinely available to everyone is to change the code restrictions and the thought patterns that build streets for cars, then "accommodate" cyclists and pedestrians afterwards.

Car-dominated streets can restrict choices, especially for the 20 percent of our population who are too old, too young, or too poor to drive, by not

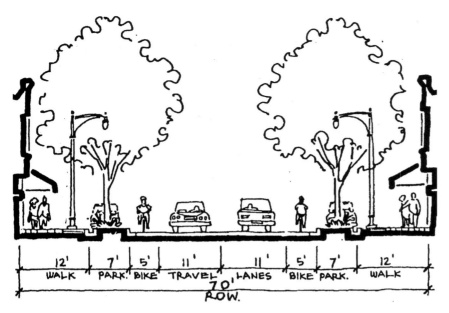

12' WALK | 7' PARK. | 5' BIKE | 11' | TRAVEL 70' LANES ROW. | 11' | 5' BIKE | 7' PARK. | 12' WALK

This cross-section of a street design for a commercial strip shows that clear "lanes" for various users have been provided. On-street parking also helps ease parking requirements and may help slow through traffic.

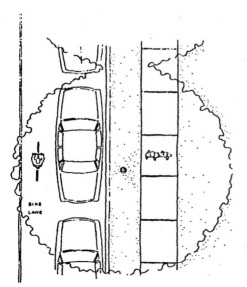

TRAVEL | 5'-0" BIKE LANE | 7'-0" PARKING | 5'-0" TREE LAWN | 6'-0" SIDEWALK | VARIES RESIDENTIAL SETBACK

BIKE LANE

A parkway containing trees, along with a lane of parking, helps shield pedestrians from traffic. As is clear from the bottom drawing, the trees also provide shade for the pedestrians, parked cars, and bicyclists. They would also certainly enhance the aesthetics of the streetscape.

allowing them the options to safely and conveniently get around on their own. Furthermore, those who do drive often tend to the transportation needs of nondrivers, such as chauffering children to the park or to school, or driving an elderly parent to the pharmacy.

Some specific code items that interfere with the goal of a multimodal street system are: no sidewalk requirements, excessive street widths, excessive speed limits, no coordinated bike routes, poor pedestrian crossings, excessive curb return radii, and poor street connectivity.

4.1 Solution: Revise Street Standards

Often, street standards for a community must be totally reworked in order to accommodate smart development principles and make streets multimodal. In other cases, existing streets and neighborhoods may already be well-designed for alternate modes. The key principle to follow in designing streets is balance—ensuring the safety and quality of the street environment for all users.

Street planners have a variety of tools to encourage multimodalism, and local development codes should be modified to allow their use. Connectivity requirements, the concept of shared street space, "skinny" street standards, mapped-out pedestrian and bicycle networks, lower speed limits, and corner bulb-outs are some examples of things that make the streetscape more multimodal. New street standards should be a combined effort of residents, emergency service providers, businesses, pedestrian and bicycle advocates, and other groups affected by the street.

4.2

4.2 Strategy: Transit, Bike, and Pedestrian Connectivity

Smart development encourages people to take alternative modes— riding transit, biking, or walking—and has multiple safe routes to get to many destinations. In neighborhoods that adhere to the smart development model, a person can leave the car at home and take a short walk to the bank machine, ride the bus to a community shopping center, or pedal a bike to a nearby park. Interconnected streets shrink distances between points and make destinations easily accessible by any method of travel. People still have the opportunity to drive when traveling longer distances, but better connections make the choice of an alternative mode for shorter trips much more appealing.

4.2 Obstacle: Physical Barriers; Out-of-Direction Travel

Poor connectivity often forces people to drive, restricting the viability of other methods. Many conventional street patterns are designed as a series of unconnected streets, funneling all traffic in a single direction and creating only one option for travel. Cul-de-sacs and other dead-end streets stretch distances for all travelers but are particularly difficult for those who do not drive. In some commercial areas, connections between adjacent buildings can be so poor that patrons return to their cars, drive back out to the arterial road, travel a few hundred feet to the adjacent

parking lot, and park again to reach the neighboring building. In residential areas, children are unable to walk to school, not because the distance is too great, but because there is only one available route and it requires walking on a busy, dangerous, traffic-clogged street.

4.2 Solution: Internal Connectivity Standards; Cul-de-Sac and Block Length Maximums; Sidewalk Requirements

Cul-de-sacs and other dead-end streets hinder connectivity and should be avoided wherever possible. Even when they are allowed, planners should attempt to make continuous, nonvehicular connections between streets. Building codes should be revised to mandate connectivity within neighborhoods, to build streets that provide continuous and generally more comprehensible routes to more destinations.

To quantify the connectivity of an area's streets, planners are beginning to use a standard ratio: street links divided by street link ends. The more links that exist relative to dead-ends, the more connectivity. This number is useful for comparing levels of connectivity between neighborhoods in different areas and can be the basis for setting standards for new development.

Shorter blocks also encourage pedestrian activity by shrinking the perceived distances between destinations and enabling people to cut through to get where they are going. A reasonable average block perimeter is 1,300 to 1,800 feet, a distance scaled to pedestrians. Finally, and obviously, requiring sidewalks on all potential pedestrian routes will make walking safer and more convenient.

In some commercial areas, connections between adjacent buildings can be so poor that patrons return to their cars, drive back out to the arterial road, travel a few hundred feet to the adjacent parking lot, and park again to reach the neighboring building

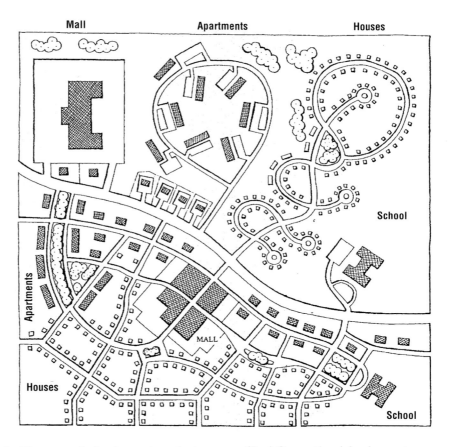

(Top) Conventional development with poor connectivity: travel requires use of the collector street, causing congestion and discouraging pedestrians and cyclists. (Bottom) Smart development with interconnected street system, allowing a variety of transportation options and shorter trips.

Collector Street

Collector Street

Local Street

Local Street

Shopping Center

Arterial Street   Arterial Street

(Left) Conventional development with limited and circuitous route options requiring travel on busy collector streets. (Right) Smart development with many options for pedestrians, bicyclists, and motorists.

4.3 Strategy: Transit-Supportive Development

Transit-supportive or transit-oriented development supports a number of smart development principles, including providing people with more transportation options. Common sense and travel studies show that people who live closer to transit will be more likely to use it, so development built adjacent to or very near a bus or rail stop will help boost transit ridership and reduce the need for automobile travel. Since residential demand for parking is lower in areas close to transit centers, developers can seize the opportunity presented by land savings and public infrastructure investment to build at higher densities. Living close to transit also gives greater choices to those who drive and offers an ideal environment for those who do not.

4.3 Obstacle: Proximity to Transit Lines not Recognized in Zoning and Development Codes

The public investment of a transit line creates opportunities for new kinds of development. Yet, if zoning regulations do not recognize this potential, underbuilding can occur and fewer people have access to transit. Sparsely populated residential and commercial areas near transit stations squander a valuable public resource and investment, and make transit attractive to fewer people.

Some cities have established transit "overlay zones" where densities are required to be higher within a quarter-mile walk from a fixed-route transit stop. This allows more intense development to occur along transit lines.

4.3 Solution: Mandate Transit-Oriented Development Along Transit Corridors

Some cities have established transit "overlay zones" where densities are required to be higher within a quarter-mile walk from a fixed-route transit stop. This allows more intense development to occur along transit lines. Transit-oriented development is an ideal, low-impact solution for accommodating population growth since transit helps mitigate the major negative effects of more people: increased traffic. To be sure that the considerable expense of maintaining a transit line is not wasted on sparse, unsupportive land-use policies, higher-density development should be required in these overlay zones.

5. DETAILED, HUMAN-SCALE DESIGN

5.1 Strategy: Compatibly Designed Buildings

A great deal of opposition to new construction and infill development comes from people who fear that new development will be incompatible with their neighborhood's character. If development to most people means cheaply built, inappropriate, or disharmonious buildings in their neighborhood, they will naturally resist any new construction. Smart development promotes new buildings that add variety while fitting with the existing neighborhood in their appearance, whether height, roof pitch, or building materials.

5.1 Obstacle: Too Abrupt Transitions Between Zones

The worst examples of incompatible building styles are frequently found on the border of zoning boundaries. On one side of the boundary is a detached, single-family home, and on the other side is an eight-story apartment building—both acceptable within their zoning requirements but uncomfortable neighbors. The cause of such abrupt changes is the recognition of the difference between zones as a line, rather than a transitional area. As long as the code has a particular set of requirements for one side of the street or zoning district boundary, and a different set of requirements for the other, the trend will continue.

5.1 Solution: Density Transitioning; Midblock Zoning District Lines; Building Height Limitations

A way to moderate the jarring effect of a zone change is to allow a transition from one to another—to encourage a mix of building types within one block on either side of the boundary. This will allow the densities and building heights to

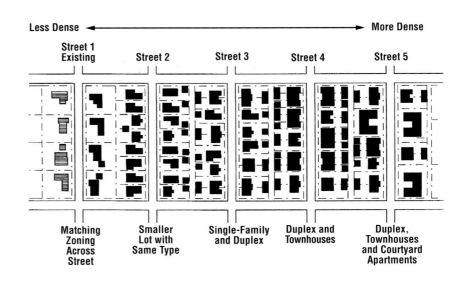

The following principles of compatible building types make it possible for a limited range of buildings to be built on the same street. The basis for compatibility is similar building massing along the street front, not exceeding the width and height of a large house. Positioning car storage well behind the front of the building (20 feet) is critical to the success of such a street. With multifamily buildings, alleys reduce the visual impact of cars by storing them to the rear.

A: 60-foot maximum continuous building frontage.

B: 15-foot minimum aggregate sideyard.

C: 25-foot minimum courtyard break in contiguous project.

D: 10-foot maximum variation in setback. For infill projects, the setback is the average setback of buildings within 300'.

E: Parking limited to the rear of the lot when alleys are not feasible (minimum 20 feet behind the building front).

Similar building types allow denser development. New housing on Street 1 has lot sizes within 10 percent of the exisiting single-family lots across the street. It also has the same front and side setbacks and the same heights. Garages are still accessible from the front but are now set behind the new houses. On Street 2, the lots are smaller but the type is still detached single family. On Street 3, duplexes are added, and on Streets 4 and 5, townhouses and apartments are introduced. All the types place parking to the rear of the lot, thereby allowing architectural elements such as doors, windows, and porches to establish street harmony.

Less Dense ◄──────────────────────────► More Dense

Street 1 Existing	Street 2	Street 3	Street 4	Street 5

Matching Zoning Across Street	Smaller Lot with Same Type	Single-Family and Duplex	Duplex and Townhouses	Duplex, Townhouses and Courtyard Apartments

gradually work up to the new level, without it happening all at once. Drawing the boundary midblock, along the rear lot line of buildings, is another method to mitigate the effect of a new building type. Finally, placing a limit on building heights prevents developers from building towers adjacent to bungalows.

5.2

5.2 Strategy: Compatibly Designed Buildings
See the benefits of compatibility discussed in the previous section.

5.2 Obstacle: No Design Guidelines for New Buildings
Conventional building types, not accustomed to mixing with one another, typically have a poor level of compatibility within neighborhoods. For the past several decades, different housing types and uses were separate from one another and needed not fit in with any other buildings. Builders and architects lost touch with the concept of compatible design, one they had used for centuries. In the absence of an outward-looking view of neighborhood harmony, buildings became inwardly focused with little relationship to the other structures in the area. When placed in older neighborhoods, these introspective houses look exceptionally awkward, out of place, even disrespectful of adjacent buildings. Often, though, they are cheaper and easier to build, so without guidance they continue to sprout up in areas in which they do not fit visually.

5.2 Solution: Incorporate Compatibility Guidelines
New and old buildings can be compatible, and residential and commercial development can share the same space area. To assure the public that these can peacefully coexist, compatibility provisions should be written into the code. Guidelines should be spelled out for roof pitches, window heights, materials, and spacing. Street frontage character is particularly important for smart development and encourages: similar heights and widths of buildings; car storage behind the building fronts; main entries, windows, and porches oriented to the street; and similar setbacks. Of these guidelines, rear parking storage and a similar building massing are important enough that they might be codified as requirements. Overall, establishing basic standards for compatibility reduces resistance to new building types and uses in an existing neighborhood.

Compatibility provisions should be written into the code. Guidelines should be spelled out for roof pitches, window heights, materials, and spacing. Street frontage character is particularly important for smart development and encourages: similar heights and widths of buildings; car storage behind the building fronts; main entries, windows, and porches oriented to the street; and similar setbacks.

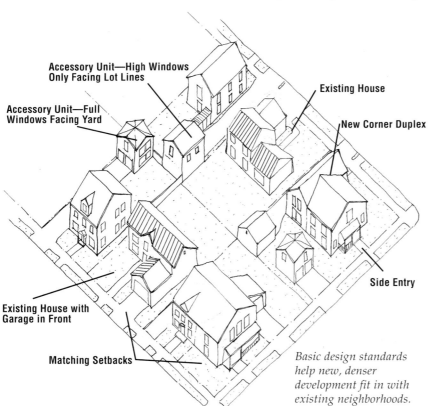

Accessory Unit—High Windows Only Facing Lot Lines

Accessory Unit—Full Windows Facing Yard

Existing House

New Corner Duplex

Side Entry

Existing House with Garage in Front

Matching Setbacks

Basic design standards help new, denser development fit in with existing neighborhoods.

5.3

5.3 Strategy: Pedestrian-Friendly Streetscapes (Commercial Districts)
Before the era of the large, auto-oriented shopping center, commercial development historically

oriented its buildings flush with the pedestrian walkway, giving merchants maximum visibility to passersby. Making commercial activity friendly to pedestrians has been an extraordinarily successful merchandising model throughout history— first with open markets, then main streets, and now the pattern is mimicked in the interior design of shopping malls.

Bringing the scale of commercial street design back to pedestrians encourages people to walk and attracts people to these areas. At the same time, a healthy, pedestrian-oriented streetscape can improve business for the merchants in the commercial district.

On business streets where on-street parking is scarce, 50 percent of the lot frontage is required to be built to the front lot line. Visible lots to the side, not the front, of the building help attract passing traffic.

5.3 Obstacle: Street Standards Overemphasize Autos; Designs Discourage Walking

Once retailers began catering almost exclusively to their customers who arrived by automobile, the model for commercial development changed. Buildings were set far back from the street, separated by vast parking lots directly in front of the building. To gain the shopper's attention for these new kind of stores, window displays were replaced with enormous signs meant to be visible by swiftly passing cars. Drive-through businesses and acres of free parking made it even easier and more practical to reach commercial activity by car.

The quick rise of automobile-oriented commercial development was disastrous for the pedestrian. Vast spaces between buildings, poor pathways to and from destinations, no sidewalks, speeding traffic, and a loss of aesthetic interest discouraged all but the most determined walkers from arriving on foot. Eager to copy the successful suburban shopping center model, Main Street districts began to permit the construction of buildings and streets that encouraged car use at pedestrian expense. On-street parking disappeared, parking lots proliferated, buildings retreated from their sidewalks, and main entrances turned away from the street.

Bringing the scale of commercial street design back to pedestrians encourages people to walk and attracts people to these areas. At the same time, a healthy, pedestrian-oriented streetscape can improve business for the merchants in the commercial district.

5.3 Solutions: Building Orientation; Location of Parking Lots; Shared Access Driveways; 80 Percent Frontage Rule for Main Street Commercial; 50 Percent for Commercial Streets; Coordinated Lighting, Signs, and Utilities; Street Trees; Limit Location of Drive-Through Lanes

Smart development codes help make commercial streets attractive, convenient, and safe for pedestrians, cyclists, and motorists alike, while accommodating the parking and loading requirements necessary for commercial viability. Commercial buildings that support smart development principles should provide an interesting and safe environment for pedestrians, encouraging walk-in business and connecting with the surrounding community. There is a need for codes that allow for the pedestrian-friendly commercial street model as well as the front-parking-lot, strip mall model.

The corner store, the main street, and the commercial street are three basic types of commercial areas crucial to smart development. For maximum pedestrian friendliness, in all three models, buildings should have little or no setback from the street; parking lots should be located behind the building if possible and to its side if not; lighting and signs should be at a scale appropriate to pedestrians and not cars; continuous, connecting sidewalks with street trees, furniture, and pedestrian-scale ighting should be required; and curb cuts should be kept to a minimum by requiring shared access.

Main Street shops present a continuous storefront along the street with windows and doors that face the sidewalk. Main Streets are at the edge of residential neighborhoods and have on-street parking with additional small parking lots behind the buildings. For a successful, interesting pedestrian environment, at least 80 percent of the street frontage must be buildings, yet there should also be a prohibition against long stretches of blank walls that face the street. Where practical, codes should be modified in Main Street districts to allow for certain commercial uses of the sidewalk, such as sidewalk sales or small cafe tables.

A corner store with on-street parking in front.

There is an inseparable link between the orientation of the main shop door toward the street and on-street parking in front of the building. Without some kind of parking in front of the store, the possibility for a store's success is marginal. Main Street standards should not be required, then, if on-street parking is prohibited.

Commercial streets also are located at the edges of residential neighborhoods but are larger in scale and face major streets that lack on-street parking. For these buildings, the rear of the lot holds the bulk of the parking and side lots fill in the rest, while parking is forbidden between the store and the street. A minimum of 50 percent of the street frontage should be buildings, again, with restrictions prohibiting long stretches of blank walls. Main entries to buildings must face the street, or at least at the corner closest to a side parking lot.

5.4

5.4 Strategy: Pedestrian-Friendly Streetscapes (Residential)
Residents in smartly developed neighborhoods feel comfortable and safe walking. Whether just out for a stroll or on the way to a particular destination, residents can walk around their community and enjoy an attractive, interesting environment that welcomes them. Walkers bring more safety, more opportunities for communication among neighbors, and easy opportunities for recreation.

5.4 Obstacle: Street Standards Overemphasize Autos; Design Discourages Walking
In their zeal to accommodate the automobile, newer housing developments frequently ignore the needs of the pedestrian. Large, blank, unfriendly garage doors face the street, houses sit so far back from the street that they are hardly visible, and sidewalks are altogether missing. The pedestrian environment in many areas is so uninviting, uninteresting, or unsafe that

walkers are regarded as suspicious or abnormal.

5.4 Solution: Require Sidewalks; Limit Setbacks; Place Garages at Rear; Allow Porch or Bay Window Encroachment; Coordinate Lighting and Utility Placement

Certain code changes can make residential zones more amenable to pedestrians, and more pleasant for all users. With few exceptions, continuous sidewalks should be required. Limiting front yard setbacks brings houses closer to the street, creating a comforting feeling of enclosure for the pedestrian and providing visual interest. Re-

Blank walls create an unfriendly pedestrian environment.

quiring garages to be set back further than the house prevents an unbroken line of blank garage doors facing the street, and discourages "two-car garage with house" style architecture. Allowing porches or bay windows to encroach slightly into the front setback makes the area more visually interesting for pedestrians. Coordinated lighting and utilities also make a more pleasing and inviting streetscape.

5.5

5.5 Strategy: Quality Architectural Design

The attraction of older neighborhoods, and the reason so many people want to live in some of them, is the quality of the architecture. A building crafted and designed to attract interest benefits not just its owner, but the whole neighborhood. Visually interesting buildings add to the quality and permanence of an area, giving it a strong local identity and foundation as a community.

5.5 Obstacle: No Incentive to Provide Amenities

Codes often are written to provide a baseline, to set out the absolute minimum a builder must do to comply with the law. Since they are written as restrictions—things builders cannot do—regulations do not encourage the construction of buildings that have true quality and character, and often any attempt to do so makes the application or design process more complicated. Since it is invariably less expensive and less time consuming to build lower-quality, bland buildings, developers will choose that route—the path of least regulatory resistance.

Smart development streets provide attractive, lively places to meet.

5.5 Solution: Density Bonuses for Amenities

A smart development could establish a clear list of amenities—porches, bay windows, roof gables, etc.—and reward developers who incorporate those elements by allowing them to build at higher densities. In effect, the density bonus compensates developers for building more attractive and sometimes more costly housing by permitting them to extract more value from a property. Such a system creates higher-quality buildings for the public to enjoy and generates a higher rate of return for the developer.

A smart development could establish a clear list of amenities—porches, bay windows, roof gables, etc.—and reward developers who incorporate those elements by allowing them to build at higher densities.

6. IMPLEMENTATION

6.1

6.1 Examining the Development Review Process

When reviewing development codes, governments should look beyond particular changes and pay careful attention to the overall process. Removing code obstacles to smart development projects will eliminate the need for variances to accommodate them, saving time for both planners and developers. Integrating smart development principles into the code creates opportunities for builders to move forward with innovative projects if they wish, without engaging them in a lengthy development review process. Nevertheless, a code can still discourage smart development if approval for such projects requires months of waiting and mountains of paperwork. In brief, smart development projects should not be penalized for innovation with delays and uncertain outcomes.

Process changes that encourage smart development should be directed specifically at smart development projects; that is, projects that meet certain criteria or performance standards based on the principles outlined in this report would automatically clear the process hurdles that would otherwise slow it down.

Because of the nature of many smart development projects, they may deviate from the traditional approval process and be subject to complications or delays. The most common, process-related problems faced by smart development projects today are: too many requirements for variances or conditional use permits, lengthy or complicated planned unit development ordinances, and overly discretionary design review processes.

6.1 Process Obstacle: Onerous Procedures for Variances, Conditional Uses

As discussed above, smart development projects are often infill projects, buildings on irregularly shaped parcels that may have environmental resources or other constraints that have caused developers to pass over the land in the past. Regulatory expectations for a standard, homogeneous development pattern may clash with the physical characteristics (i.e., slope, wetlands, riparian areas) of a particular parcel of land. Nevertheless, since most codes currently establish exact dimensions for lot width, depth, and size, and most zones also have maximum density and minimum lot area requirements, smart development projects must apply for variances in order to build on such parcels. Strictly applying these requirements to infill often results in less buildable land than if developers had the flexibility to cluster development or to average dimension requirements within overall density maximums.

The purpose for removing code obstacles is to reduce the need for variances to accommodate smart development projects. However, this may not be possible in all cases. Because of their unusual shape or size, infill lots

When reviewing development codes, governments should look beyond particular changes and pay careful attention to the overall process. Removing code obstacles to smart development projects will eliminate the need for variances to accommodate them, saving time for both planners and developers.

often call for different building plans than neighboring houses. To make the project fit the available space, a site planner may need to design the building in such a way that it varies from the applicable zoning code. For example, in order to give the front porch adequate depth without taking away from the square footage of the house, a designer might ask that the steps encroach three feet into a 20-foot front setback. Unfortunately, the only way to get permission for even the most minor changes in some development codes may be to enter into a long, complicated, and expensive variance process. The prospect of months of delays and additional paperwork thus discourages developers from pursuing smaller-scale projects.

6.1 Solution: Allow Administrative Approval for Minor Adjustments

While a variance, and the process for acquiring one, is appropriate when a plan calls for significant changes from the existing laws, minor changes could bypass this process, or at least the requirement for a public hearing. A planning director could be empowered to approve adjustments in the code within a defined range (e.g., adjustments may not exceed a 20 percent difference). A jurisdiction may also want to cap the number of administrative adjustments without a public hearing (e.g., no more than three adjustments per project).

This kind of code flexibility could have helped the developer of a proposed single-family residential infill project in southeast Portland, Oregon. Initially, the developer wanted to build four units of housing on a 19,200-square-foot parcel of land. However, the zoning code for the area called for minimum lot sizes of 5,000 square feet per unit, leaving him 4 percent shy of the land area requirement for a four-lot partition. Despite the fact that the parcel had street frontage on two sides, the developer was forced to divide the land into only three lots. These three lots are now 28 percent larger than originally planned, and both the city and the developer have lost the opportunity for an additional unit of housing. More flexibility in the code would have allowed this project—if it met all of the other code standards—to go through.

In another process change, Vancouver, Washington, has created a fast-track permitting process to encourage mixed-use development. Meeting certain requirements for mixed use entitles the project to an "Expedited Development Review Process," placing the applicant on a priority list.

6.2

6.2 Examining the Planned Unit Development (PUD) Process

See the benefits of reviewing the development process described under Strategy 6.1.

6.2 Process Obstacle: Onerous Planned Unit Development (PUD) Requirements

Many smart development projects involve the mixing of housing types and different commercial and residential uses that are either prohibited or not addressed in development codes. As a result, developers must either apply for variances or enter into a planned unit development process, both of which can be time consuming and costly.

For larger infill projects, codes sometimes implicitly encourage development that makes inefficient use of land. Strict standards designed to protect the public from bad projects can also have the effect of discouraging good ones. New or innovative strategies for making the most of available land, such as changing the mix of building types or mixing uses, are sometimes expressly forbidden, unless a motivated developer has applied for a planned unit development.

While a variance, and the process for acquiring one, is appropriate when a plan calls for significant changes from the existing laws, minor changes could bypass this process, or at least the requirement for a public hearing. A planning director could be empowered to approve adjustments in the code within a defined range (e.g., adjustments may not exceed a 20 percent difference). A jurisdiction may also want to cap the number of administrative adjustments without a public hearing (e.g., no more than three adjustments per project).

6.2 Solution: Improved PUD Ordinances

Allowing limited, small-scale commercial buildings in residential areas or multifamily buildings in certain commercial areas (see the discussion of mixed use above) eliminates the need for many PUD applications. For large-scale projects, specific code changes to the PUD process can guide smart development and relieve some of the regulatory work for both developers and planning officials. For example, instead of simply mandating a minimum or maximum density for a development, a community could allow higher densities in exchange for specified amenities, such as a public park, pedestrian, or bicycle facilities, design features, or a site for a school. Code language would need to clearly state the nature and extent of the amenities and the bonus earned for each.

6.3 _____

6.3 Flexibility in the Design Review Process

See the benefits of reviewing the development process described under Strategy 6.1.

6.3 Process Obstacle: Discretionary Design Review Process

A great deal of community opposition to new development projects, smart or otherwise, is based on design issues. In response, many communities have instituted design standards, often with a design review hearing separate from land-use approvals. While many communities have instituted design guidelines and a design review process to try to protect against bad designs, the design review process can serve to bog down or delay projects. Vague design standards that can be broadly interpreted invite uncertainty and controversy. Again, this level of uncertainty may encourage developers to take the path of least resistance, leading to mediocre building and site designs that preserve the status quo.

6.3 Solution: Dual-Track Design Review Process

One approach to improving design review is to create a dual-track process that allows the developer to choose from two options:

1. Adherence to prescribed and detailed specific design standards
2. A more flexible design review process based on performance guidelines

This approach requires the community to create two sets of development standards. One set of prescriptive standards is defined in terms of distances, heights, density, and other precise and quantifiable standards that can be applied through an administrative process without public notice or hearings. The other set of performance guidelines outline community objectives and are more flexible and likely to result in exciting and innovative design, but do require public notice and hearings.

The key is providing certainty and flexibility. The developer of a smaller, straightforward project can proceed with administrative review, provided the project meets specific standards. A more elaborate or complex project can go before a design review board to provide the design flexibility that some developers or architects prefer.

The key is providing certainty and flexibility. The developer of a smaller, straightforward project can proceed with administrative review, provided the project meets specific standards. A more elaborate or complex project can go before a design review board to provide the design flexibility that some developers or architects prefer.

Chapter 5

A Community Program for Change

A decision that these principles are worth employing should not be limited to only professional staff, but should represent a consensus of the key community stakeholders—planning commissioners, developers/builders, professional consultants, neighborhood and community activists, and elected officials.

The assessment of the current code should clearly identify whether the obstacles to smart development are procedural, matters of substance, or simply a matter of providing clarity as to intent.

The initial step in any effort to incorporate the principles of smart development into local plans and standards is to decide which of these smart development principles are appropriate for the community. A decision that these principles are worth employing should not be limited to only professional staff, but should represent a consensus of the key community stakeholders—planning commissioners, developers/builders, professional consultants, neighborhood and community activists, and elected officials. Local citizens must see these principles as a way to improve choice, convenience, compatibility, and connections in their neighborhoods. Although one or several local champions may provide leadership in promoting these principles, ultimately there should be a broader consensus that the principles add value to a community.

Once there is agreement that smart development is worth pursuing, the next step is to decide what to do and how to do it. This begins with evaluating existing plans, codes, and standards to determine if the community's policies and implementation tools support smart development or include particular obstacles. At this stage, planners also should determine whether smart development changes can assist in implementing any state-mandated planning requirements.

This overall evaluation could stem from a comprehensive review process, such as is required during periodic review, or from the development of a specific plan element, such as a transportation systems plan or a housing policy study, that may focus on one or two smart development principles. Local citizens can be the catalysts for prompting the consideration of smart development, or it could be a developer seeking more flexibility in building a project supported by the community and responsive to smart development principles. Finally, smart development changes could be initiated by a staff member, planning commissioner, or elected official who has read or heard about examples of how they have benefited other communities.

Regardless of how change begins, broad agreement that smart development makes sense for the community is an essential element for long-term success. Having decided which principles to pursue, local officials can then move ahead to institute changes, either piecemeal or wholesale.

The assessment of the current code should clearly identify whether the obstacles to smart development are procedural, matters of substance, or simply a matter of providing clarity as to intent. In some cases, changes may have to address all three areas, or the assessment may show that only one of these areas needs to be addressed to remove obstacles. Furthermore, communities may choose to "experiment" with some of these ideas on an interim basis, retaining some degree of oversight to see how these principles work in practice. Based on their own experiences, and as builders, planners, and citizens reach a greater level of comfort and understanding, communities could then move to eliminate all obstacles.

Once a community decides it wants to consider smart development changes, a review process should be established. The key precept to be followed in designing such a process is that it be inclusive of as many interests as possible. This provides an opportunity to both inform and educate the public as well as obtain input and feedback.

The following approach might be used to conduct a review and establish smart development recommendations. It should be noted that this approach may not apply if the review was initiated by a developer who is proposing code changes to remove obstacles.

Step 1: Set Workplan; Identify and Involve Stakeholders

1. Develop a work program and schedule for the review.

2. Evaluate whether staff resources are adequate or if outside consulting assistance will be needed to supplement staff resources or to provide a third-party perspective.

3. Identify key community stakeholders with an interest in removing obstacles. These should include local elected officials; the planning commission; representatives of the local development community (i.e., lenders, developers, builders and their planning or architectural consultants); representatives of neighborhood, community, civic, environmental or other organizations; the local media, and others with an interest.

4. Conduct interviews/meetings with these stakeholders to inform them of the efforts and to seek their input on obstacles, concerns, and opportunities that should be addressed. At this point, you may also want to provide a background briefing to the media.

5. Set up an advisory committee made up of stakeholders to obtain review and feedback in subsequent steps of the process.

Step 2: Identify Code Obstacles; Outline Possible Solutions

1. Conduct a review of codes and procedures to identify obstacles to smart development, using this report as a guide.

2. Meet with the advisory committee to discuss obstacles and appropriate solutions.

3. Brief the planning commission on the obstacles and potential solutions, and obtain their feedback. If possible, brief the elected officials on project status.

4. Prepare a draft set of proposals with clear explanations of alternatives. Be sure to describe why code changes would result in positive community benefits. Review the draft with the advisory committee and modify it, if necessary.

Step 3: Review Solutions; Adopt Changes

1. Provide an opportunity for public review and comment of the draft proposals through an open house, a display, and, if appropriate, presentations to interested organizations. Brief the media on the effort to help publicize the open house.

2. Based on all the comments received, revise the draft recommendations. Review the new recommendations with the advisory committee and the

planning commission. Depending on whether there is controversy surrounding the revised draft, you may decide to send the revised draft out to the original group of stakeholders to get their comments in writing.

3. Present the revised draft at a work session with local elected officials.

4. Prepare a final draft. Review it with the advisory committee and obtain their recommendations.

5. Present the final report with advisory committee recommendations at a public hearing of the planning commission. The planning commission recommends actions to the elected officials.

6. Final action is taken at a public hearing of the elected officials, and changes are made to the code to reflect those actions.

EXECUTIVE SUMMARY

Smart development is "smart" because it uses land efficiently, facilitates a range of transportation choices, and attracts people. By using land efficiently, smart development minimizes infrastructure development and maintenance costs for communities. By providing a range of transportation choices, smart development reduces our dependence on the automobile, thereby protecting our future air quality, creating more affordable living situations for people, and minimizing future expenditures on road construction and maintenance. By attracting people, smart development ensures the long-term vitality of the neighborhood or district, reducing the incentives for sprawling development.

Despite these benefits and public-sector commitment to achieving them, smart development is only a small portion of recent development in Oregon. Smart development projects are often more difficult and costly to develop because of a number of barriers. These barriers can affect whether or not developers are able to successfully complete a project, and may discourage them and others from pursuing smart development in the future. The five categories of barriers listed below were identified through interviews with developers around the state.

Local Regulations

Local regulations can make "smart" development difficult. Poor or antiquated zoning, lengthy development permit approval processes, and public facilities standards designed according to conventional development patterns can discourage smart development.

Market Conditions

Smart development is an unfamiliar market for most lenders and developers and, as such, it is perceived as risky. Outdated assumptions informing current market and demographic analysis prevents developers from targeting smart development at significant groups of emerging consumers with specific needs, tastes, and preferences.

Development and Process Costs

Local fees and costs for development which fail to factor in the benefits of smart development, increasing land and construction costs, and a shortage of suitable infill sites makes smart development more expensive and complicated.

Financing

A lack of comparables, the secondary financing market, and bank structures and procedures can make securing financing for smart development projects difficult. In addition, excessive parking requirements which are often imposed by lenders add expense and may conflict with the goals of the project.

Community Involvement

Both open land development and infill projects have met with community opposition. A lack of public education often translates into continued community opposition, even when the community supports the overall goals of smart development.

THE SYMPOSIUM

This publication presents the barriers to smart development so the accompanying symposium can be a catalyst for removing those barriers. Industry leaders attending the symposium will develop strategies to overcome the barriers to smart development and commit to a series of action steps for removing the barriers in their industry. This publication should be viewed as a working document that, in its final form, will include the strategies and action steps identified at the symposium for overcoming each barrier.

Top Five Barriers to Smart Development*

*This appendix is a reprint of an issue paper, produced by Livable Oregon, in preparation of the Governor's Symposium on Smart Development, which occurred on November 20, 1996, at the Benson Hotel in Portland, Oregon. It is reprinted with the permission of Livable Oregon.

INTRODUCTION

The goals of smart development are to create livable communities that use resources efficiently, are less dependent on the automobile, make good use of community centers, and fit in with the existing neighborhood structure. The result of smart development is interconnected, business-friendly neighborhoods, where people live, work and recreate. Despite these goals and public sector commitment to achieving them, smart development is only a small portion of recent development in Oregon.

Although many of Oregon's older neighborhoods exemplify smart development, it is a "new" concept in today's development industry. Because of its newness, regulatory and financial systems currently in place are not set up to accommodate it. As a result, certain barriers exist that can cause delays and increase costs. The impact of these barriers are twofold: they may frustrate developers who are trying to do smart development now, and they may discourage other builders from pursuing this form of development in the future.

This publication summarizes the regulatory and financial issues surrounding smart development as recorded in the experiences of Oregon developers who have recently undertaken a smart development project. These projects were built all over Oregon and ranged from the creation of a new downtown to a single mixed-use building. Out of conversations with these developers, five common categories of barriers emerged:

- Local Regulations
- Market Conditions
- Development and Process Costs
- Financing
- Community Involvement

These five categories include all the barriers that were recounted to us by developers describing specific development projects. The examples included in each section of this paper illustrate some of the difficulties encountered and, in some cases, the strategies employed by developers to overcome those difficulties.

While our original goal was to identify the barriers that were mentioned most often, we found that local regulations and regionally based institutions can cause variation in experiences. For example, one developer may feel that zoning codes restrict design objectives and another may find that their local government encourages smart development projects by willingly and expediently making all necessary regulatory changes. Both developers encountered barriers, but the barriers were different based on the local regulations. Such differences are difficult to quantify. Nevertheless, while regional variation impacts the relative significance of the barriers from one developer to another, all the barriers experienced by developers fit into one of the five categories.

As developers decide what types of projects to build, they assess the impact of the various barriers on their ability to complete the project on time and receive a sufficient return on their investment. Since the regulatory and lending institutions are set up to serve single-use projects or subdivisions fitting a conventional suburban pattern/design, it is often easier to build what the existing system encourages than encounter one of the above-listed barriers. One objective of the smart development project is to encourage industry leaders to break down the barriers that exist, and develop strategies that encourage more livable communities.

LOCAL REGULATIONS

Zoning and Subdivision Standards

Zoning Codes. Zoning codes can be restrictive, complicated, and unmanageable. Moreover, they can actually preclude smart development by mandating large lots, wide streets, deep setbacks, and separation of uses.

Design Requirements. Many developers argue that design requirements slow down the development and permitting process. On the other hand, many planners argue that a lack of design requirements leads to poorly designed development that can fuel local resistance to future, well-designed, smart development projects.

Development and Permit Approval Process

Innovative projects, like smart development, may take longer to gain development or permit approval if public agencies are unfamiliar with the design concepts and requirements. Developers of new "traditional" neighborhoods often seek approval under zoning regimes that are unaccustomed to such concepts and as a result they can get caught up in lengthy negotiations with the city on issues such as lot layout and street requirements. A single dwelling unit or a specific aspect of a larger project can also face delays in the permitting process if they are attempting to build something outside of current codes. For these reasons, smaller developers, unable to sustain a lengthy permit process, may choose to work within existing codes and develop in typical patterns and designs.

Public Facilities Standards

Smart development is often inhibited by local codes for public facilities that prohibit features like narrower streets, alleys, and shorter block lengths. Zero lot lines and denser development also may be complicated by the placement and capacity of public facilities, such as water meters, utilities lines, and sewers. For developers undertaking infill, existing infrastructure may not have sufficient capacity to serve increased density or it may need to be moved or rebuilt to accommodate structural changes. Furthermore, for new, denser patterns of development outside of the city center, written guidelines may not yet be available on how and where to place public facilities. Unless developers, public agencies, and utility providers are able to work in a coordinated manner, placement or upgrading of public facilities could delay or complicate development.

EXAMPLE 1. PRINCETON AND ASHLEY VILLAGES

Mixed-use residential/office rowhouses and single-family homes in neotraditional planned community, Clackamas County, Oregon

Don Oakley, developer of Princeton Village and Ashley Village, has found some permitting requirements to be in conflict with his building designs. Oakley's design calls for detached garages in alleys. This design allows front setbacks to be reduced and street widths narrowed. This design concept requires an additional step in the permitting process since a separate permit is required for the dwelling unit and another for the detached garage. Attached garages, which do not require this step, are therefore appealing to developers concerned with time and potential regulatory hassles. Local governments wishing to encourage this type of development could combine the garage and dwelling unit permit process to save the developer time and money.

51

EXAMPLE 2. WEST BEND VILLAGE

Single-family subdivision, Bend, Oregon

During the development of West Bend Village, Mike Tennant could not get the necessary approval to reduce front setbacks. As a result, he had to maintain Bend's requirement of 20-foot setbacks, even though he placed garages in alley ways instead of using a front driveway. Tennant deliberately designs his neighborhoods to

create a greater sense of community. This is done by controlling the Codes Covenants & Restrictions (regulations that govern the development) to include such things as front porches and limited fence heights which create more opportunities for conversation and interaction. However, maintaining Bend's 20-foot front setback diminished some of the community aspect of the development and limited backyard space. For his development in Baker City, the city council approved all of his requested zoning changes, which included rezoning the land from primarily industrial with limited residential to a mix of residential, industrial, commercial, parks, and some mixed live-work lots. He also got approval for alleys and narrower streets. He attributes this difference to the efforts he made to inform Baker City officials about the benefits of traditional neighborhoods, the reasoning behind the zoning changes, and the willingness of Baker City officials to consider and adopt an alternative plan.

EXAMPLE 3. JEFF FISH DEVELOPMENTS

Infill and single-family residential developer, Oregon

Jeff Fish, a developer of infill and single-family residential projects, has a parcel of land in southeast Portland that is zoned for a minimum lot size of 5,000 square feet, and is just 4 percent shy of the required square footage to allow a four-lot partition. Even though the lot has frontage on two streets and is almost 20,000 square feet, the City of Portland will not entertain the idea of partitioning it into four lots since Fish lacks certain requirements, such as lot depth and width. Fish is currently seeking approval for a three-lot partition from the city, which forces him to build on lots that are 28 percent larger than his original plan, and is not certain that he will get that approval. Fish feels that this misuse of valuable land within the urban growth boundary is in direct opposition to the goals of increasing density and encouraging infill development.

EXAMPLE 4. FAIRVIEW VILLAGE

Mixed-use residential/retail/commercial, Fairview, Oregon

Holt and Haugh, developers of Fairview Village, took an alternative approach to the development and permitting process, which required extensive planning and resources upfront, in an effort to avoid some of the lengthy delays often associated with innovative development. With an initial nod of approval from the City of Fairview for the concept, Holt and Haugh held a design charette with 100 participants, including 35 people in decision-making positions within the permitting and approval process at the state, county, and city level. The charette process resulted in a master plan and significant buy-in from decision makers, making the process of permitting, comprehensive plan amendments, and code changes much more efficient. Randy Jones of Holt and Haugh estimates that this nine-month permitting and approval process would have taken 18 months to two years had they not involved the public and all relevant decision makers early in the development process. While this was a time savings for the developer, it required significant resources and effort up front.

EXAMPLE 5. STEELE PARK

Transit-oriented, mixed-density residential Washington County, Oregon

Joanne Rice, the Washington County planner involved in the development of Steele Park, found that using zero lot lines or zero side yards created difficulties with codes and access to public facilities. During the building of Steele Park, the developer found that protecting the space that would be used for eave overhangs, gas meters, gas lines, foundations, drainage, and maintenance to the houses required added coordination during planning and construction because the buildings were so close.

Summary of Local Regulation Barriers

- Zoning and subdivision standards support conventional land-use and design and are incompatible with smart development objectives. Smart development projects require a variance in most cases.

- Development and permit approval processes support land-use and design that are incompatible with smart development objectives. Smart development projects often require negotiations and delays.

- Public facilities standards which have been developed to support conventional development patterns conflict with smart development design features and goals. Smart development projects often require a variance for street standards or added coordination or guidance for utilities and other public facilities placement.

MARKET CONDITIONS

Unfamiliar Market

Lenders and developers alike have benefited from Oregon's growth and booming housing industry. Suburban homes have been a good, low-risk investment. The relatively unfamiliar market of smart development does not offer this same track record. Furthermore, most of Oregon's developers take on only a small number of projects each year. For example, 400 out of 500 Portland-area builders build fewer than eight houses a year. Smaller developers are apprehensive about smart development projects since failure to attain stable financing or difficulty leasing units could have a huge financial impact on their businesses. Lenders are apprehensive about financing smart development projects without successful track records for this type of development, especially when the developer lacks experience and significant credit history.

Marketing and Changing Demographics

Previous market studies which predicted a demand for three-bedroom suburban homes may no longer be accurate. Nevertheless, detached, single family homes in conventional subdivisions continue to be financed and sold. Without good, up to date demographic and market information and an understanding of the target markets for smart development products, developers, builders, and lenders may be unsure of market demand for smart development. However, a move from traditional suburban tract housing to smart development requires a thorough understanding of consumer needs, preferences and ability to pay. Developers have been criticized for incorrectly estimating market price, for over looking demographic trends, and for generally lacking sophisticated marketing techniques.

EXAMPLE 1. MORNINGSIDE HEIGHTS AND MORNINGSIDE TERRACE

Infill subdivision, Salem, Oregon

Bob Hamilton, builder of Morningside Heights and Morningside Terrace, notes that the people who purchase his homes are second- or third-time, more sophisticated buyers. Their homes do not attract attention from first-time buyers and as a result they have found the market slow. While this is partly a result of the higher prices on their homes, he also believes that first-time buyers do not understand the benefits of smart development or are unaware that this kind of development exists.

EXAMPLE 2. DAWSON PARK PLACE AND ALBINA CORNER

Mixed-use residential, Portland, Oregon

Peter Wilcox, Executive Director of Portland Community Design (PCD), developer of Albina Corner, a 48-unit mixed-use commercial/retail/residential project, and Dawson Park Place, a seven-unit infill rowhouse development, believes that builders should not only build for the median homeowner/tenant, but can also successfully build for a particular segment of the market. At PCD, Wilcox has pursued this strategy and his quick sales/leasing are testimony to the success of this approach. At Dawson Park Place, PCD and its joint venture partner, HOST Community Development Corporation, sold six out of seven homes within two weeks of completion. Using intuition instead of a formal market analysis for the Dawson Park Place project, he found that there is strong demand for rowhouses from a particular segment of the market. Prior to building Albina Corner, PCD conducted extensive market analysis which showed that their target market included 9,000 people, mostly seniors and single moms, who are potential leasers of urban, mixed-use housing in northeast Portland. The accuracy of the market analysis was confirmed when 95 percent of the units at Albina Corner were leased 45 days prior to completion.

Summary of Market Condition Barriers

- The "newness" of smart development in today's development market makes it a risk for lenders and developers when compared to the good track record of conventional suburban housing and commercial development.

- Current assumptions about demographics and the market which support conventional development persist may no longer be accurate. A lack of good, up to date market information prevents lenders and developers from identifying products to serve emerging market niches which may be more demanding of smart development.

DEVELOPMENT AND PROCESS COSTS
Infrastructure, Services, Utilities

Development Fees. To meet the needs of new residents, development fees are imposed on builders to ensure that sufficient parks, schools or other public improvements are included in the proposed development. Infill developers are often charged the same development fees as open land developers even if the park or service already exists in the area where development will occur.

Comparable Cost Categories. Extending utility lines, paving roads, and expanding sewers are costs directly related to new development outside of urbanized areas. However, since these costs are paid for by the full district or region, through taxes and increased rates, they are often not directly considered a cost of a specific development project. This comparison makes new development outside of the urban center look less expensive than infill. It also raises equity considerations since people living in urban centers, where services are already established, are actually subsidizing sprawling development by sharing in the costs.

This type of analysis may also fail to use comparable cost categories or to include the full range of cost/benefit decisions. Cost/benefit categories, such as pollution, use of public transportation, increased sense of community, and quality of design, are generally not considered when weighing the costs and benefits of development.

Land and Construction Costs

Land and construction costs are rising at a rapid rate in Oregon. This can make developers less innovative, more tied to old product lines, and even more conscious of the bottom-line financial return. As a result, emphasis on design and planning may be overlooked for cost savings. Rising costs may also make developers more wary of taking on smart development projects since they are less certain that they can correctly estimate costs and complete the project within budget.

Shortage of Suitable Sites and Assemblage of Sites

Multiple landowners and scattered parcels of available land can make infill development difficult. Developers who undertake large infill projects may have to build several smaller projects on scattered parcels of land. This can lead to higher per-unit costs since fixed costs can be spread over fewer units. The barrier of land assemblage could cause developers to purchase a single large tract of undeveloped land outside of an urban area rather than undertaking infill projects that require time-consuming assembly of land. Moreover, infill sites often require additional time and money during the development process for negotiation of environmental constraints, zoning issues, and concerns of neighboring interests.

EXAMPLE 1. GRESHAM CENTRAL TOWNHOUSES AND FLATS

Transit-oriented, 80-95 unit, residential development, Gresham, Oregon

When they began to develop this project, which is adjacent to Tri-Met's light rail line and would require a lot of infrastructure development, Gresham Central Development sought public assistance in the form of Congestion Mitigation Air Quality-Transit Oriented Development (CMAQ-TOD) funds to help cover the costs. (CMAQ-TOD funds are federal funds administered by the Oregon Department of Transportation for public improvements for projects that are transit supportive.) When additional infrastructure costs exceeded the committed public funds, they had to seek additional CMAQ-TOD funding. The additional costs included a two- story parking structure, additional design features for the buildings, fees for storm water and sewer systems, and a sprinkler system. While the developer was eventually able to finance the project and begin construction, significant public financing to cover the costs associated with the project were required.

EXAMPLE 2. CITY LIFE

Owner-occupied, 18-unit, infill development, Portland, Oregon

Working on City Life, REACH Community Development learned that one of the challenges to infill development is fitting a complicated development program onto a tight site. City Life, located in an established residential neighborhood in southeast Portland, is comprised of 18 units, including rowhouses, a duplex, and courtyard units, on a 40,000-square-foot lot. Although the City Life Steering Committee considered more than 15 sites, the most suitable site still presented significant challenges. It required a zone change and a comprehensive plan amendment, and it was located next to an industrial lot. Since they selected a tight site and built at densities two times greater than typical, REACH found it essential to meet early with the city to determine such issues as utility and stormwater drainage requirements, which were then incorporated into the initial design and pro forma.

EXAMPLE 3. ANKENY WOODS

Transit-oriented, affordable housing development, Portland, Oregon

Human Solutions, a nonprofit, affordable housing developer found it difficult to assemble a large enough site for their Ankeny Woods project to meet density requirements for the area. They eventually purchased one vacant property and two adjacent properties with houses on them. As a non-profit, affordable housing developer, they had an additional advantage over private developers in that they were able to get some adjacent sites from Multnomah County and achieved their goal of a one acre site. A second challenge for the developer was getting the required street improvements to extend the street to the site. While Human Solutions would be responsible for the costs of the improvements on 430 feet of the street, they were more concerned about getting the other property owners to agree to bear the costs of their portion of the street improvements. Through connections with the city's Bureau of Housing and Community Development, they were able to apply and receive a 70% subsidy for their portion of the street improvement costs and for the other property owners as well. Human Solutions believes that without that subsidy, the other property owners would not have agreed to cover the costs of the street improvement. While Human Solutions was able to overcome the challenges of site assemblage and infrastructure improvements, they noted that private developers would have more difficulties if they didn't have the same subsidies to help them bear the costs.

Summary of Development and Process Cost Barriers:

- Development fees do not take into account the cost/benefit of different types of development for the community. Smart development is often characterized by features that are less burdensome on community infrastructure and services, yet the fee structure does not take this into account.

- As a "new" type of development, smart development appears more risky for developers when faced with rising land and construction costs. Design features of smart development add additional cost and, therefore, risk for the developer.

- Suitable infill sites are difficult to identify and, at best, are accompanied by challenges that take additional time and process steps to correct.

COMMUNITY INVOLVEMENT
Community Opposition
Both open land development and infill projects have met with community opposition. Infill projects are especially vulnerable to community opposition simply because they tend to have more neighbors. Citizens fear that the new development will decrease their property values and increase crime, traffic, noise, pollution, and competition for services. Often it is uninformed opposition that leads the charge. For example, residents may oppose narrow streets on the grounds that they are unsafe, when it actually has been shown that skinny streets slow traffic and increase pedestrian safety. While active involvement by neighborhood residents and local businesses can mitigate this problem, community opposition may reemerge even after the project is underway.

Lack of Public Education
Throughout the development process, the public has an opportunity to express support or opposition for a specific project trying to gain approval. Through this process, the public influences the type of development that makes it to the marketplace. A community that is aware of some of the benefits of smart development, such as reducing pollution, increasing the use of public transportation, and making better use of natural resources, may be better prepared to participate in the approval process. Without a significant educational campaign that informs communities about the need for smart development, neighborhoods may continue to support development that is conventional and familiar.

EXAMPLE 1. CENTRAL BETHANY

Mixed-use residential/retail/commercial, Bethany, Oregon

The developer, Roy Kim, has faced community opposition head-on. Community members were uncomfortable with the planned density of Central Bethany and held the project up in appeals for a long period of time, which was expensive for the developer. As a result of his community outreach and extensive educational efforts, Kim now finds that the community believes in the plan and wants to make sure it happens as promised. While this is a positive step, Kim may now face new challenges from an overinvolved community group.

SUN CREST CONCEPTUAL DEVELOPMENT PLAN

Mixed-density residential, Corvallis, Oregon

Sun Crest, a development plan for 612 dwelling units on 102 acres, has encountered significant citizen opposition. A transfer of density in accordance with Corvallis' Comprehensive Plan allowed the developer, Wolfgang Dilson, to set aside 30 acres of open space for preservation while increasing density on the remaining 72 acres, to maintain a total density of six units per acre. Sensitive to the concerns of surrounding neighbors, Dilson designed the development so that single-family homes will be adjacent to existing single-family homes in the neighborhood. A mixture of attached and detached homes will be located away from existing development. The planning commission's approval of the project was appealed by citizens and a neighborhood association on grounds that it exceeded maximum-density requirements for the area, would generate a high volume of traffic, and was incompatible with the surrounding single-family neighborhoods. According to the City's community development director, the Sun Crest plan met the land-use goals of Corvallis' Comprehensive Plan and the appeals against it were unfounded. The City Council eventually denied the appeals and upheld the planning commission's approval of the Sun Crest Plan. Subsequent to that decision, a individual citizen appealed to the state's Land Use Board of Appeals where approval of the project was again upheld.

While the project was ultimately approved at each level, the appeals caused lengthy delays for the developer.

Summary of Community Involvement Barriers:

- Community opposition can cause delays in the development approval process.
- Lack of public understanding about smart development goals leads to continued opposition to smart development.

FINANCE

Lack of Comparables

Before undertaking a development project, lenders want to look at comparable projects in the marketplace to assess the level of risk and set the terms of the loan package. Smart development projects, whether infill or open land development, often lack exact or close comparables. In addition, smart development projects can be more expensive than neighboring housing, due largely to design quality. Appraisers basing their rates on neighboring housing that is older or less innovative in design may not offer an appraisal value equivalent to the full value of the house. As a result, the loan amount, derived from the appraisal value, will not reflect the full value of the house and buyers will be required to put more money down. Developers trying to appeal to an emerging market, such as smaller families and empty nesters, with smaller homes, rowhouses, or other innovative products face a lack of comparables for these products and lower appraisal values. Appraisers could increase smart development appraisal values by considering design quality, increased use of public transportation, a greater sense of community, and reduced pollution as positive economic benefits.

Achieving Secondary Funding

Banks can lend beyond what they possess in assets and reserves by selling mortgages in the secondary market. If a project with some level of perceived risk is not sold in the secondary market, few banks will want to assume financial responsibility. The secondary market does not tend to underwrite condominiums, townhouses, live-work units, co-ops, cohousing, mixed-use developments, and the like. Thus, if a lending institution does not sell the project in the secondary market, and it is uncertain about the financial solvency of the product, it will be less likely to make the loan.

In addition, Fannie Mae, the largest mortgage guarantee company, has a "pass-through" requirement that makes banks financially responsible for the project through foreclosure of the asset. Banks do not like to own real estate and, if they are responsible for smart development projects in cases of foreclosure, they will require strong comparables and a proven track record to ensure that they can recover their investment.

Bank Structure Incompatibility with Mixed-Use Projects

Lending institutions have separate departments for handling commercial, residential, and industrial loans. Smart developers that combine these uses are required to negotiate with each department, which can double or triple the amount of time and paperwork required. Working with multiple persons at a bank can lead to increased project costs, delays, and opportunities for miscommunication. In the case of foreclosure, it is not certain which bank department should take over the property and what procedures should be followed. This can cause the bank to be less interested in lending on a project.

Parking

Developers may face pressure from regulators and lenders to provide excessive parking even if the surrounding land is expensive, difficult to procure, or unavailable. Some developers eager to secure financing might concede to lenders who insist on more parking as part of the project. As a result, driving may be emphasized over other modes of transportation. Likewise, lenders and regulators may pressure developers of affordable housing to provide parking even if that cost puts the rent/purchase price out of the reach of the target market.

EXAMPLE 1. CITY LIFE

Owner-occupied, 18-unit, infill development, Portland, Oregon

City Life incorporated three types of housing in one planned unit development (PUD). Because of its innovative nature, the project lacked adequate comparables and made it difficult for the appraisers to value the property. As a result, both the construction appraisal and the initial individual home appraisals came in low. The amount the construction lender was able to lend based on the appraised value was less than what was needed to build the project. REACH Community Development, the community development corporation that developed the project, secured a bridge loan from the City of Portland to fill this gap. Individual appraisals that came in low were reappraised by a second appraiser, which resulted in a higher value for the properties and helped facilitate the selling of the homes.

EXAMPLE 2. TUALATIN MEWS AND VILLAS ON THE LAKE

Downtown "hoffices" and rowhouses, Tualatin, Oregon

Don Silvey, developer of Tualatin Mews and Villas on the Lake in the newly developed downtown Tualatin Commons, found that the financing community is not equipped to handle mixed-use development. His rowhouses, which are purely residential, were financed with relative ease, while his "hoffices," which offer commercial/retail space downstairs and residential space upstairs, required significantly more work. The mixed-use project was more difficult to finance since secondary market backing could not be obtained. Fannie Mae encumbers secondary financing by only guaranteeing mixed-use projects that are 20 percent commercial. Ultimately, Silvey shopped around until he found a lender who would keep his loan in house and not sell it on the secondary market.

EXAMPLE 3. FAIRVIEW VILLAGE

Mixed-use residential/retail/commercial, Fairview, Oregon

Developing a financing strategy to fit the banking structure, which is highly segmented, may be necessary to obtain financing, but it may lower appraisal values. For Fairview Village, the banks would accept appraisals only on isolated lots, rather than in the context of the total village community. While this segmented approach resulted in financing for the project, in this example it effectively reduced appraisal values by 15 percent.

EXAMPLE 4. BELMONT DAIRY

Mixed-use residential/commercial/retail, Portland, Oregon

The developers of Belmont Dairy, a mixed-use project located on a commercial street in southeast Portland, wanted to limit parking by using shared parking. They felt that not only is parking expensive to provide, but, since most of their customers/tenants will walk or ride the bus, it is unnecessary. However, their lender felt uncomfortable financing this project without more parking. The bank eventually concurred but only after the developers spent hours of time and paid a consultant to generate a technical report demonstrating the feasibility of shared parking.

Summary of Finance Barriers

- Smart development projects often lack comparables, which can lower appraisals and affect the feasibility of the project.
- Banks are cautious about projects that cannot easily be sold on the secondary market. Smart development product types often mix uses and are not easily bundled for sale on the secondary market.
- Smart development is often characterized by a mix of uses that is difficult for the highly segmented banking industry to process.
- Lender requirements for large amounts of parking can be in direct conflict with goals of smart development projects.

Editor's Note: Some of the ordinances contained in this appendix originally appeared in the Oregon report upon which this PAS Report is based, and some were chosen by research associates at APA. They are arranged by the strategies outlined in the main body of this report. It is clear from the width and breadth of the communities represented in this appendix that planners, citizens, and local officials are implementing smart development strategies in settings as varied as small towns and large urban areas. The principles embodied in the strategies would seem to transcend issues of community size, geography, and even character. That so many communities have implemented such progressive strategies speaks well to the efforts of local planners and the citizens who are demanding that the planning in their community reflects their values and enhances opportunities to create neighborhoods that are people oriented rather than auto oriented and that have a distinct and recognizable character. This report and these examples are offered to those who are still beginning the process of change necessary to create communities based on these planning principles and strategies. These provisions should prove useful in crafting language for ordinance provisions and plans that will encourage smart development. As is true whenever adopting or revising a code, ordinance, or plan, jurisdictions should consult both their state enabling legislation and their staff attorney before attempting to incorporate any of these provisions into law.

Ordinance and Plan Provisions that Communities Might Use to Implement Smart Development Strategies

STRATEGY 1.1. SMALL LOT INFILL

Fairview, Oregon, Standards for a Village Townhouse Residential District

3.830 Village Townhouse Residential District (VTH)

3.831 Purpose. This district is intended primarily for attached single-family dwellings in a medium- to high-density residential environment.

3.832 Permitted Uses. The following uses and their accessory uses are permitted in a VTH district.

A. Single-family dwellings (detached)

B. Attached single-family dwellings (townhouses, rowhouses, duplexes)

C. Two-family dwellings

D. Accessory buildings, such as garages, carports, studios, private workshops, playhouses, private greenhouses, or other similar structures related to the dwelling in design, whether attached or detached

E. Parks and playgrounds

F. Family day care providers and residential homes

G. Home occupations

H. Signs

I. Accessory dwelling units shall be allowed on lots at the end units only of common-wall, lot/building sequences (rowhouses) of three or more. A maximum of one accessory dwelling unit shall be allowed on such lots. If the accessory dwelling unit occurs over the garage, the garage must be detached from the main dwelling unit. (This provision will expire on November 15, 1999, unless renewed by that time by the Fairview Planning Commission and City Council.)

3.833 Conditional Uses. The following uses and their accessory uses are permitted as conditional uses in a VTH district after approval of the planning commission:

A. All conditional uses in the R–4 district with the exception of mobile home parks and golf courses

3.834 Development Standards

A. *Density.* VTH lots shall be no less than 2,000 square feet and no greater than 4,000 square feet in area. Corner lots in the VTH districts may be larger than 4,000 square feet but shall be no more than 5,500 square feet in area.

B. *Lot dimensions.* Lots in VTH districts shall have a minimum width of 20 feet and a minimum depth of 70 feet.

C. *Lot coverage.* The total of all structures shall cover no more than 70 percent of any lot.

D. *Height.* Buildings within this district may not exceed 35 feet in height.

E. *Setbacks.* Dwelling unit front facades shall be set back from the right-of-way for a distance of either 10 or 15 feet. Sides of units may have a setback of zero feet from the property line on both sides of the lot. The rear facade shall be set back a minimum of 15 feet from the rear property line.

F. *Garages*

  1. Attached garages with front access are not permitted on lots accessible from an alley or rear parking lot.

  2. Attached garages or detached garages may have a minimum setback of zero feet from the rear property line, provided the front facade setback requirement in Section 3.834.E is met and provided there is a minimum of eight feet of separation between adjacent garages. Provided further, where the garage vehicle entrance is perpendicular to the alley, a four-foot setback shall apply.

  3. Attached or detached garages may have a side yard setback of zero feet. Lots not accessible from the rear may have attached, front accessed garages. Such garages must have an equal or greater setback than the front facade and shall have a separate door for each vehicle space with a maximum of two garage doors each having a maximum width of 12 feet.

STRATEGY 1.2. ENCOURAGE INFILL DEVELOPMENT ON LARGE LOTS

Martin County, Florida, Community Redevelopment District

Section 35-2.29 CR

A. *Purpose and Intent.* The CR district is established to provide an alternative zoning procedure that may be used to implement Comprehensive Growth Management Plan policies by providing opportunities for traditional neighborhood design and mixed residential and commercial uses in redeveloping areas. The CR district is set up to preserve and revitalize older residential neighborhoods and commercial areas by allowing modifications to base zoning district and other applicable regulations and by establishing special design standards for development, in accordance with a community plan for redevelopment and conservation. Appropriate locations for the establishment of CR districts shall be limited to existing developed areas, such as commercial downtowns, which could benefit from revitalization in the form of specific long-range planning, innovative development options, and community improvement programs.

STRATEGY 1.3. COORDINATED DEVELOPMENT

Newberg, Oregon, Specific Plan Subdistrict Process

425 Purpose. The purpose of the Specific Plan (SP) subdistrict is to allow the development and approval of specific plans in the city. A specific plan is a master plan applied to one or more parcels in order to coordinate and direct development in terms of transportation, utilities, open space, and land use. The purpose is also to streamline the development process and encourage development according to the specific plan. Specific plans are intended to promote coordinated planning concepts and pedestrian-oriented mixed-use development.

426 Plan Development and Approval Process

A. *Initiation.* The process to establish a specific plan shall be initiated by the city council. The planning commission or interested property owners may submit requests to the council to initiate the specific plan process. If owners request initiation of a specific plan process, the council may require an application fee to be paid to cover the cost of creating the plan.

B. *Steering committee.* The city council shall appoint a steering committee to guide development of the plan. The steering committee shall include persons representing affected property owners, neighbors, and the community at large.

C. *Draft plan.* The steering committee shall develop a draft plan that shall be submitted to the planning commission and council for review, modification, and approval.

D. A specific plan shall include text and a diagram or diagrams that specify all of the following in detail:

1. *Plan objectives.* A narrative shall set forth the goals and objectives of the plan.

2. *Site and context.* A map of the site and context shall indicate existing land use, slope, and natural features.

3. The distribution, location, and extent of the uses of land, including open space and parks, within the area covered by the plan (Land Use Plan).

4. The proposed distribution, location, and extent of major components of public and private transportation, sewage, water, drainage, and other essential facilities proposed to be located within the area covered by the plan and needed to support the land uses described in the plan.

5. Standards and criteria by which development will proceed and standards for conservation, development, and utilization of natural resources, where applicable.

6. The plan shall identify the existing property ownership.

7. A circulation/transportation plan shall be included that identifies the proposed street pattern including pedestrian pathways and bikeways. Design standards and street cross-sections shall be included.

8. *Hearings and decisions.* The planning commission shall hold a public hearing on the plan and shall make a recommendation to the city council. The city council shall have final approval authority. The hearing process to be followed shall be the same as that set forth for zone changes pursuant to Sections 598–608. If the specific plan affects land outside the city limits, provisions and procedures required under the urban growth management agreement with Yamhill County shall also be met.

427 Approval Criteria. Adoption of the specific plan and its related subdistrict shall be based on compliance with the zone change criteria.

428 Plan Implementation

A. *Overlay subdistrict.* The specific plan shall be implemented as a zoning overlay subdistrict. If the plan applies to land outside the city limits, the SP Plan Classification District shall indicate where the SP overlay zone will be applied upon annexation. The specific plan shall be adopted as an exhibit to the SP overlay zone subdistrict and the SP overlay plan district.

B. *New construction.* New construction under site review or building permit review shall meet the special development and design standards of the specific plan.

C. *Priority of standards and procedures.* Unless otherwise noted, the standards and procedures of the specific plan overlay subdistrict shall supplement and supersede standards and procedures of the zoning ordinance.

429 Amendments and Adjustments to the Specific Plan. Amendments to the specific plan may be either major or minor amendments.

A. *Definitions–Minor and Major Amendments*

 1. Major amendments are those which result in any of the following:

    a. A change in land use

    b. A change in the circulation/transportation plan that requires a major street (collector or arterial) to be eliminated or to be located in such a manner as to not be consistent with the specific plan

    c. A change in the development standards

    d. A change in the planned residential density

    e. A change not specifically listed under the major and minor amendment definitions.

 2. Minor amendments are those which result in any of the following:

    a. Changes related to street trees, street furniture, fencing, or signage that were approved as part of the specific plan

    b. A change in the circulation/transportation plan that requires a local street, easement, or pathway to be shifted more than 50 feet in any direction

    c. A change in the utility plan other than what would be necessary for authorized adjustment of lot lines.

B. *Major amendments.* A major amendment to a specific plan shall be processed as a comprehensive plan amendment. The amendment shall meet the criteria of Section 427, above. In addition, findings must demonstrate that the change will not adversely affect the purpose, objectives, or functioning of the specific plan.

C. *Minor amendments*

 1. *Community development director decision.* A minor amendment to a specific plan may be approved by the community development director. The director's decision shall include findings that demonstrate that the change will not adversely affect the purpose, objectives, or functioning of the specific plan. Notice of the director's decision and an opportunity to appeal the decision to the city council shall be provided to all owners of land within or abutting the SP plan overlay district in question.

 2. *Appeals.* Any person aggrieved by the decision of the director may appeal the decision within 10 days of the mailing of the decision and shall file the appeal on a form provided by the director. An appeal fee shall be charged. Upon filing the appeal, the community development director shall set a hearing before the city council. The hearing shall be at the next available meeting provided proper notice is made consistent with Section 766 of the zoning ordinance.

D. *Authorized adjustment of lot lines.* As part of the final platting process, the community development director is authorized to grant adjustments to proposed lot lines consistent with flexible density standards (if included) as part of the specific plan subdistrict. Notice of the adjustment is not required.

430 Interim Development. To encourage platting in conformance with the specific plan, the following modifications to street, subdivision, and development standards may be granted outright without notice by the community development director.

A. *Temporary dead ends.* Temporary cul-de-sacs or vehicle turnarounds where a through street will eventually be provided. Due to the their temporary nature, the dimensions and improvement requirements for these cul-de-sacs and turnarounds may vary from standards set forth in the subdivision ordinance.

B. *Temporary street improvement.* Half-width or three-quarter-width streets may be provided temporarily to access lots where a full street will eventually be provided when all abutting lots are developed.

C. *Tracts.* Tracts of land that do not meet specific plan density requirements may be created and developed when it is demonstrated that the tracts can be developed in accordance with the specific plan in the future. If construction occurs on the tract, it shall be done in a manner that will meet specific plan development standards when full improvements are provided.

431 Specific Plan Development Standards. Development standards for specific plans are listed below. The standards shall be used in conjunction with the specific plan adopted as an exhibit to the SP overlay subdistrict. This section is intended to be amended as new specific plans are adopted.

A. *The Northwest Newberg Specific Plan*

1. The Northwest Newberg Specific Plan Final Report . . . is hereby adopted by reference. The development standards listed in this section shall take precedence over those listed in the report. If ambiguity exists, the zoning ordinance shall govern.

2. *Permitted uses and conditional uses.* The permitted and conditional uses allowed under the SP subdistrict shall be the same as those uses permitted in the base zoning districts. . . .

3. *Street and pedestrian pathway standards.* Street and pedestrian pathway standards are as follows:

	ROW	Paved Surface
Local street	60 feet	32 feet
Collector street	74 feet	36 feet
Pedestrian connection	16 feet	6 feet

Five-foot bike lanes shall be provided along collector streets. Five-foot sidewalks shall be provided along local and collector streets. A six-foot-wide planter strip shall separate the sidewalk and the collector street. Local streets shall be designed as through streets. Cul-de-sacs shall be used only if a through street can not be developed.

4. *Setbacks*

a. *Area 1 setbacks.* Minimum and maximum front setbacks for structures shall be met in Area 1 of the Specific Plan. Residential structures shall be no closer nor further from the front property line than as follows:

	Minimum	Maximum
Porch	10 feet	25 feet
Dwelling	15 feet	25 feet (without porch)
Garage or Carport	20 feet	None

The front of a garage may not be closer to the property line that the front of the house unless each front on different streets.

b. *Area 2 setbacks.* Special minimum front setbacks for residential structures shall be met in Area 2 of the Specific Plan. No maximum setback is required. Front setbacks are as follows:

	Minimum	Maximum
Porch	10 feet	None
Dwelling	15 feet	None
Garage or Carport	20 feet	None

c. *Interior setbacks.* Interior yard setbacks shall be the same as the base zone.

d. *Commercial and institutional setbacks.* Except as set forth in subsection 7 below, setbacks for commercial and institutional uses shall be set by the base zone or as otherwise required in the zoning ordinance.

5. *Street trees.* Street trees shall be required along all streets. One tree shall be required for every 40 feet of street frontage or fraction thereof (e.g., a lot with 50 feet of frontage will provide two street trees; a lot with 100 feet of frontage will provide three street trees). Trees shall be provided in accordance with the list of trees included in the specific plan. Trees shall have a minimum of a 1.5- or 1.75-inch caliper tree trunk and shall be balled and burlapped or boxed.

6. *Residential density.* Residential density is governed by the SP overlay subdistrict. The maximum allowed density is set by the number of lots depicted on the [land-use plan]. . . . Additional standards follow:
   a. Minimum lot size
      Single-family dwellings: 5,000 square feet

      Attached dwellings: 3,750 square feet

   b. Maximum density
      LDR districts: set by the specific plan (averages 4.4 dwelling per acre)

      MDR districts: 8.8 dwellings per acre

   c. *Flexible minimum density requirements.* The following standards may be applied at the time of platting:
      i. Lots may be increased to 7,500 square feet

      ii Lot size may be increased above 7,500 square feet, provided that the overall density of the original parent parcel at the time of specific plan approval remains at or above 80 percent of the original planned density, the overall density of the combined parcels may be used for the calculation. For these calculations, the planned density for LDR areas shall be assumed to be 6.5 dwelling units per acre (5,000-square-foot single-family lots) and MDR at 8.8 dwelling units per acre.

7. *Building orientation.* All development shall be oriented to a local or collector street. Orientation shall be achieved by the provision of an entry door fronting upon the street with a direct sidewalk connection from the door to the public sidewalk.

[Editor's note: Standards for commercial development follow but have not been included here. See samples below for examples of standards that promote mixed-use neighborhoods and healthy commercial districts.]

STRATEGY 1.4. BETTER USE OF DEEP LOTS

Boulder, Colorado, Provisions for Two Detached Dwellings on a Single Lot

9-3.2-16. Two Detached Dwellings on a Single Lot

A. *Standards.* In an MR-E, MR-X, HZ-E, HR-E, or HR-X district, two detached dwelling units may be placed and maintained as principal buildings on a lot which fronts on two public streets other than alleys, if the following conditions are met:

   (1) Each principal building shall have adjacent to it and convenient to use by its occupants a landscaped area of at least 120 square feet, with no side less than ten feet in length, and with privacy screening. The screening requirement may be met through any combination of building placement, landscaping, walls, or fencing;

   (2) A uniform landscape plan shall be provided and executed, and all existing trees over three inches in caliper measured four inches above the ground shall be preserved, unless this requirement is waived by the city manager for good cause;

   (3) In the MR zoning district, one parking space is required for each principal building. In the HR-E zoning district, for the second principal building, one

bedroom requires one off-street parking space, two bedrooms require one and one-half spaces, three bedrooms require two spaces, and four or more bedrooms require three spaces.

Required parking is provided on the lot convenient to each principal building. Any two parking spaces fronting on an alley which are adjacent to each other shall be separated from any other parking spaces by a landscaped area at least five feet wide and as deep as the parking spaces;

(4) Privacy fencing or visual buffering of parking areas is provided;

(5) Each principal building has separate utility services in approved locations;

(6) All utilities are underground for each principal building unless this requirement is waived by the city manager for good cause;

(7) New principal buildings are compatible in character with structures in the immediate vicinity, considering mass, bulk, architecture, materials, and color. In addition, the second principal building placed on a lot shall meet the following requirements:

(a) The second floor shall not exceed 60 percent of the area of the first floor;

(b) Only two floors, exclusive of lofts or towers with floors no larger than 100 square feet in the aggregate, shall be above grade;

(c) The above-grade floor area shall not exceed 1,200 square feet. The floor area for a single-car detached garage which does not exceed 240 square feet and is a minimum of five feet from another principal structure may be added to the 1,200 square feet if the additional floor area does not exceed the FAR in subparagraph (d) below; and

(d) The FAR shall not exceed 0.45, calculated as follows:

(i) All above-grade floor area, garages, accessory structures, courts, and basements that are located below a floor level which is more than 30 inches above the natural grade shall be included in the floor area; and

(ii) If a subdivision request for the lot is part of the application under this section, the new lot upon which the building will be located shall be the basis for the FAR. If there is no subdivision application, the smaller building site for FAR calculations shall be 40 percent of the lot, or such larger portion not to exceed 60 percent as the city manager shall approve as constituting a reasonable lot consistent with the requirements that would have to be met were the lot to be subdivided; and

(e) If the second principal building is the rear building, the roof eaves exclusive of dormers on the alley face of the building shall not be more than 12 feet above grade;

(f) If the second principal building is the rear building, the exterior wall surface area on the alley face of the building over nine feet above the grade of the alley shall not exceed 75 percent of the area of that face below nine feet. Exterior wall surface area on the alley face shall include all surfaces which face the alley steeper than a 12/12 pitch which are within 10 feet of the wall surface closest to the alley; and

(g) The building height of the second principal building, if it is located at the rear of the lot, shall not exceed 25 feet.

(8) Setback requirements shall be modified as follows:

(a) New principal buildings shall maintain the side yard setback requirements for the MR-E zoning district of Section 9-3.2-1, "Schedule of Bulk Requirements," B.R.C. 1981, regardless of the zoning district in which the lot is located;

(b) At least 10 feet shall be maintained between the principal buildings;

(c) The front yard setback requirement of Section 9-3.2-1, "Schedule of Bulk Requirements," B.R.C. 1981, shall be met for the front building;

(d) If there is an alley at the rear 20 feet or more in width, then there shall be no rear yard setback requirement for the rear building;

(e) If the alley is less than 20 feet wide at the rear for lots which have frontage on two public streets, the rear yard setback for the rear building shall be five feet; and

(f) If there is no alley at least 15 feet wide for lots which have frontage on two public streets, the rear yard setback requirement of Section 9-3.2-1, "Schedule of Bulk Requirements," B.R.C. 1981, must be met for the rear building.

B. *Subdivision.* If two principal buildings are to be or have been constructed on a lot pursuant to subsection [A. Standards] above, such lot may be subdivided, upon application, into two lots, one for each principal building, if the following requirements are met:

(1) The smaller of the two lots is at least 40 percent of the square footage of the original lot;

(2) The lot line created between the two principal buildings shall be substantially perpendicular to the side lot lines.

(3) The subdivision in all other respects complies with the subdivision requirements of Chapter 9-5, "Subdivisions," B.R.C. 1981, except as those requirements are modified by this section concerning street frontage, density and open space requirements, and setbacks; and

(4) The subdivision agreement recites all of the conditions of this section as continuing limitations on future buildings and uses of each lot, and that one or both lots, whichever may be the case, are nonconforming lots containing nonconforming buildings whose change to or expansion of use, lot, or building is subject to the provisions of this title or their successors concerning nonconformity.

STRATEGY 1.5. LESS LAND FOR STREETS

The Eugene, Oregon, Local Street Plan: Proposed Local Residential Street Standards

The Eugene Local Street Plan proposes a broader range of local residential street types and includes narrower street cross sections than are currently allowed. Local residential streets that are as narrow as possible have several benefits to the community.

Narrow streets cost less to build and maintain. Less road base is needed and less surface area is paved. This results in lower material and labor costs. City of Eugene staff estimates than an eight-foot reduction in local street width results in at least a 10 percent reduction in paving, sidewalk, and finishing costs.

Narrow streets reduce the negative impacts of stormwater runoff. Paved streets are impervious surfaces that prevent the filtration of stormwater into the ground. Therefore, streets increase the volume of stormwater runoff, which can cause flooding, erosion, and habitat destruction, as well as reducing the groundwater supply. Excess paving also causes increased pollution of surface waters as a result of contaminants from the roadway surface entering the stormwater system. The City of Eugene Stormwater Management Program recognizes reduced street widths as a means of reducing the volume of runoff.

Narrow streets reduce the negative environmental impacts of street construction. A narrow street cross section will help minimize environmental impacts by requiring less land than a wider street. For improvements on existing unimproved streets, narrow widths will reduce the need to remove existing plants and trees.

Narrow streets encourage more efficient land use. The land saved by using narrow street designs can be used for other purposes, including housing, landscaping, and open spaces.

Narrow streets increase traffic safety. Narrow street designs will discourage the use of local streets by through traffic and help reduce traffic volumes and speeds. This will help to create quiet, safe, residential streets with low traffic volumes and speeds. . . . Lower vehicle speeds will also reduce the severity of pedestrian [injuries from] automobile accidents. According to the Center for Urban Transportation Research, approximately 55 percent of accidents are fatal to the pedestrian when vehicle speeds are 30 mph and over, while only 5 percent are fatal to the pedestrian when vehicle speeds are 20 mph or lower.

Narrow streets improve neighborhood character. The positive environmental, land-use, and traffic safety impacts of narrow streets all work to improve the character and livability of residential neighborhoods. The 1980 Bucks County, Pennsylvania, publication, *Performance Streets*, recognized that the purpose of local streets should be "not solely to move traffic safely and efficiently, but to ensure that the needs of people for a residential neighborhood that is quiet, safe, pleasant, convenient, and sociable are met as well."

Two of the most frequent concerns expressed by residents are high traffic speeds and nonlocal traffic searching for a shortcut through a neighborhood. Often, both are a result of poor local street design. As a result, the typical remedy is increased traffic control and enforcement. Even with the additional control, it is difficult to manage the problem for a sustained period of time. The best solution is to create geometric street designs that self-enforce the desired levels of speed and traffic volumes.

Traffic volumes on local streets are typically low and on-street parking demand can vary, depending on the density of adjacent development, the vehicle ownership rates of local residents, and the amount of on-site parking provided on lots fronting the street. The design and appearance of local streets should be consistent with the intended function of the street. Generally, the design standards for these streets should promote relatively narrow widths, short lengths, and alignments that encourage slow traffic speeds and discourage through traffic.

Generally:

Local street lengths should be short. Shorter street lengths also create smaller visual elements. Instead of focusing their attention far down the road, drivers become more aware of pedestrian, bicycle, and other nearby activity that causes drivers to reduce speed.

Streets should be designed with gentle curves and changes in grade. If drivers can see for several blocks down a street, they tend to increase their speed. Curves, changes in grade, and other design features interrupt the sight line of the road into smaller visual elements and cause drivers to slow down.

Traffic calming features, such as curb extensions, traffic circles, and medians should be used to encourage slow traffic speeds. Curb extensions, traffic circles, and most other traffic calming features are regarded as permanent devices intended to discourage speeding and should be included in initial street design when appropriate. Speed bumps and humps are considered retrofit solutions, applicable to the improvement of existing unimproved streets, and should not be included in new designs, except at the discretion of the city's traffic engineer.

Low-volume streets should be aligned to form three-way intersections when possible. In residential areas, many of the streets have the same width and appearance; thus, at intersections, there is no distinct differentiation between the streets and no apparent right-of-way assignment. As a result, accidents increase whenever two continuous streets meet at a four-way uncontrolled intersection. In these situations, it is usually necessary to assign right-of-way by the use of yield or stop signs.

On the other hand, three-way intersections create an inherent right-of-way assignment that significantly reduces accidents, without the use of traffic controls. Three-way intersections should be used for low-volume residential streets when possible. If used, three-way intersections should be offset a minimum of 150 feet to avoid . . . jog intersections.

A low-volume street that intersects a higher order street, such as a collector, should be aligned with another street to form a four-way intersection. When a low-volume street intersects a higher order street, there is a clearer understanding for the driver about right-of-way assignments. Because of the higher traffic volumes on the main street, right-angle, four-way intersections are encouraged at these locations and are often regulated by traffic control devices.

Avoid creating intersections on low-volume streets that require traffic control devices, such as stop signs. Reserve stop signs for locations where accident problems exist, where visibility of an approach is limited, and where traffic volumes are high.

Alleys. These streets provide secondary access to residential properties where street frontages are narrow; where the street is designed with a narrow width to provide limited on-street parking; or where alley access development is desired to increase residential densities.

Street Function:	Provides rear-yard access to individual properties and alternative utility placement area.
Average Daily Traffic:	Not applicable
Right-of-Way Width:	20 feet
Paving Width:	16 feet for two-way traffic
	12 feet for one-way traffic
Parking:	No parking within the right-of-way
Setbacks:	Fences and structures set back a minimum of two feet behind property line
Sidewalks:	None
Curb and Gutter:	Inverted curb for private alleys (asphalt);
	No curb for public alleys (concrete)

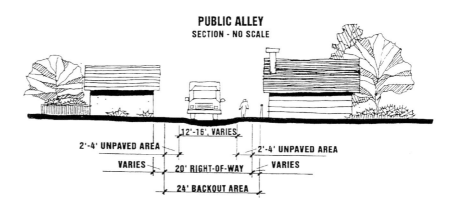

PUBLIC ALLEY
SECTION - NO SCALE

2'-4' UNPAVED AREA   12'-16', VARIES   2'-4' UNPAVED AREA
VARIES   20' RIGHT-OF-WAY   VARIES
24' BACKOUT AREA

Access lane. This street is designed for primary access to a limited number of residential properties. On this street type, the residential environment is dominant and traffic is completely subservient. Access lanes can be constructed as cul-de-sacs, loop streets, or short streets connecting two other streets. Access lanes generally serve 25 or fewer homes, and traffic volumes are low (less than 250 Average Daily Traffic) with a design speed of 25 mph.

Street Function:	Residential property access serving no more than 25 dwelling units
Average Daily Traffic:	Less than 250 Average Daily Traffic
Right-of-Way Width:	40 feet to 55 feet
Paving Width:	21 feet to 28 feet
Travel Lane:	One 14-foot travel lane ("queuing street")
Parking:	Options for parking on one side, and parking on both sides
Sidewalks:	Required on at least one side of 21-foot streets and both sides of 28-foot streets. Both curbside and setback sidewalks are permitted. The section drawings below show setback sidewalks.
Curb and Gutter:	Yes. Inverted curbs permitted under certain conditions.
Connectivity:	Bulb or turnaround area connects to adjacent street with bicycle/pedestrian accessway where feasible. Loop and short-length connecting streets connect to a higher order street at both ends.

21' ACCESS LANE
SECTION - NO SCALE

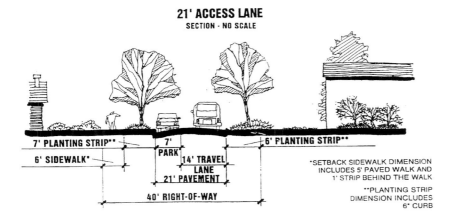

7' PLANTING STRIP**
6' SIDEWALK*
7' PARK
14' TRAVEL LANE
21' PAVEMENT
40' RIGHT-OF-WAY
6' PLANTING STRIP**

*SETBACK SIDEWALK DIMENSION INCLUDES 5' PAVED WALK AND 1' STRIP BEHIND THE WALK

**PLANTING STRIP DIMENSION INCLUDES 6" CURB

28' ACCESS LANE
SECTION - NO SCALE

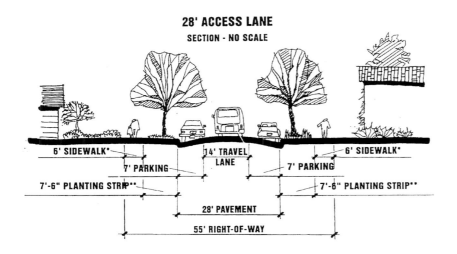

6' SIDEWALK*
7' PARKING
7'-6" PLANTING STRIP**
14' TRAVEL LANE
6' SIDEWALK*
7' PARKING
7'-6" PLANTING STRIP**
28' PAVEMENT
55' RIGHT-OF-WAY

Low-volume residential street. This street is designed for primary access to individual residential property as well as access to adjacent streets. As with access lanes, the residential environment is dominant. Traffic volumes are relative low (250 to 750 Average Daily Traffic) with a design speed of 20 mph.

Street Function:	Residential property access to individual properties and adjacent streets.
Average Daily Traffic:	250 to 750 Average Daily Traffic
Right-of-Way Width:	45 feet to 55 feet
Paving Width:	20 feet to 28 feet
Travel Lane:	Options for two 10-foot travel lanes or one 14-foot travel lane ("queuing street")
Parking:	Options for no on-street parking, parking on one side, and parking on both sides
Sidewalks:	Setback sidewalks required on both sides of the street
Curb and Gutter:	Yes
Connectivity:	Connects access lanes to medium-volume residential streets and other higher order streets

20' LOW-VOLUME RESIDENTIAL STREET
SECTION - NO SCALE

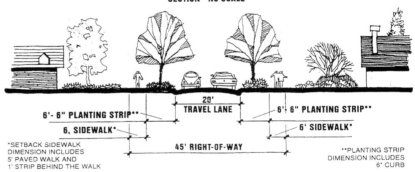

21' LOW-VOLUME RESIDENTIAL STREET

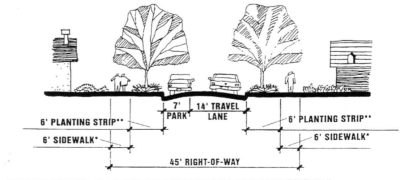

*SETBACK SIDEWALK DIMENSION INCLUDES 5' PAVED WALK AND 1' STRIP BEHIND THE WALK
**PLANTING STRIP DIMENSION INCLUDES 6" CURB

28' LOW-VOLUME RESIDENTIAL STREET

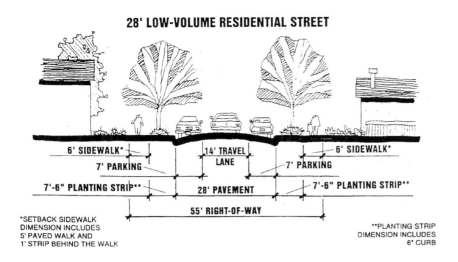

6' SIDEWALK*

7' PARKING

7'-6" PLANTING STRIP**

14' TRAVEL LANE

6' SIDEWALK*

7' PARKING

7'-6" PLANTING STRIP**

28' PAVEMENT

55' RIGHT-OF-WAY

*SETBACK SIDEWALK DIMENSION INCLUDES 5' PAVED WALK AND 1' STRIP BEHIND THE WALK

**PLANTING STRIP DIMENSION INCLUDES 6" CURB

Medium-volume residential street. This street is designed for primary access to individual residential properties, to connect streets of lower and higher function, and to access the major street network. These streets are designed to accommodate higher traffic volumes (750 to 1,500 Average Daily Traffic) with a design speed of 25 mph.

Street Function:	Provide access in and out of residential neighborhohood
Average Daily Traffic:	750 to 1,500 Average Daily Traffic
Right-of-Way Width:	50 feet to 60 feet
Paving Width:	20 feet to 34 feet
Travel Lane:	Two 10-foot travel lanes
Parking:	Options for no on-street parking, parking on one side, and parking on both sides
Sidewalks:	Setback sidewalks required on both sides of the street
Curb and Gutter:	Yes
Connectivity:	Collects traffic from within residential areas and connects these areas with the major street network

20' MEDIUM-VOLUME RESIDENTIAL STREET
SECTION - NO SCALE

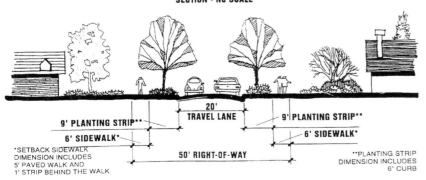

9' PLANTING STRIP**

6' SIDEWALK*

20' TRAVEL LANE

9' PLANTING STRIP**

6' SIDEWALK*

*SETBACK SIDEWALK DIMENSION INCLUDES 5' PAVED WALK AND 1' STRIP BEHIND THE WALK

50' RIGHT-OF-WAY

**PLANTING STRIP DIMENSION INCLUDES 6" CURB

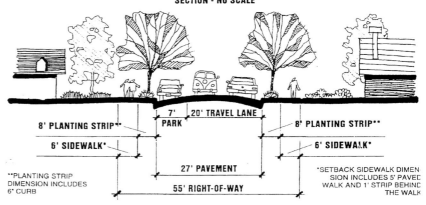

27' MEDIUM-VOLUME RESIDENTIAL STREET
SECTION - NO SCALE

8' PLANTING STRIP**

6' SIDEWALK*

7' PARK

20' TRAVEL LANE

8' PLANTING STRIP**

6' SIDEWALK*

**PLANTING STRIP DIMENSION INCLUDES 6" CURB

27' PAVEMENT

55' RIGHT-OF-WAY

*SETBACK SIDEWALK DIMENSION INCLUDES 5' PAVED WALK AND 1' STRIP BEHIND THE WALK

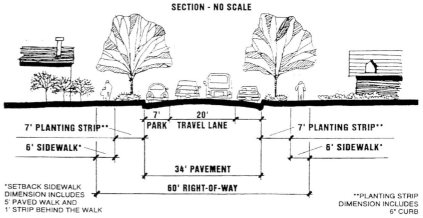

34' MEDIUM-VOLUME RESIDENTIAL STREET
SECTION - NO SCALE

7' PLANTING STRIP**

6' SIDEWALK*

7' PARK

20' TRAVEL LANE

7' PLANTING STRIP**

6' SIDEWALK*

*SETBACK SIDEWALK DIMENSION INCLUDES 5' PAVED WALK AND 1' STRIP BEHIND THE WALK

34' PAVEMENT

60' RIGHT-OF-WAY

**PLANTING STRIP DIMENSION INCLUDES 6" CURB

STRATEGY 1.6. MORE EFFICIENT PARKING USE

Boulder, Colorado, Parking Reduction Provisions

Ordinance No. 5656 (1994)

9-3.3–9 Parking Reduction

. . .

(c) *Parking reduction criteria:* Upon submission of documentation by the applicant of how the project meets the following criteria, the city manager may approve reductions of up to and including 20 percent of the parking requirements of [bulk requirements] if the manager finds that:

1. The parking needs of the use will be adequately served; a mix of residential uses with either office or retail uses is proposed, and the parking needs of all uses will be accommodated through shared parking;

2. If joint use of common parking areas is proposed, varying time periods of use will accommodate proposed parking needs; or

3. The applicant provides an acceptable proposal for an alternate mode of transportation program, including a description of existing and proposed facilities and assurances that the use of alternate modes of transportation will continue to reduce the need for on-site parking on an ongoing basis.

(d) *Parking reduction with a concurrent use review:* If a proposed use requires both a review pursuant to Section 9–4–9, "Use Review," and a public hearing, the city manager will make a recommendation to the approving agency to approve, modify and approve, or deny the parking reduction as part of the use review approval.

(e) *Assurances of the nature of the use:* If the applicant proposes to reduce the number of off-street parking spaces because of the nature of the occupancy, the applicant must provide assurances that the nature of the occupancy will not change.

Santa Monica, California, Reduced Parking Provisions

9.04.20.26.010 Purpose. A reduced parking permit is intended to permit the reduction of required automobile parking spaces for senior housing, or when shared parking, tandem parking, or in-lieu parking fees are proposed as part of any development, and under certain circumstances for landmarks and historic districts.

9.04.20.26.030 Applicability. The Zoning Administrator may grant a reduced parking permit for the following:

A. *Shared parking.* Facilities may be shared if multiple uses cooperatively establish and operate parking facilities and if these uses generate parking demands primarily during hours when the remaining uses are not in operation. (For example, if one use operates during evenings or weekdays only.) The applicant shall have the burden of proof for a reduction in the total number of required parking spaces, and documentation shall be submitted substantiating the reasons for this requested parking reduction. Shared parking shall be approved only if:

   1. A sufficient number of spaces are provided to meet the greater parking demand of the participating uses.

   2. Satisfactory evidence has been submitted by the parties operating the shared parking facility, describing the nature of the uses and times when the uses operate so as to demonstrate the lack of conflict between them.

   3. Additional documents, covenants, deed restrictions, or other agreements as may be deemed necessary by the Zoning Administrator are executed to assure that the required parking spaces provided are maintained and uses with similar hours and parking requirements as those uses sharing the parking remain for the life of the building.

B. *Senior housing.* The Zoning Administrator may approve a reduced parking permit for the reduction in the number of parking spaces required for senior citizens and senior group housing based upon findings that the proposed development is located in direct proximity to commercial activities and services, and is adequately served by public transportation systems.

C. *Tandem parking.* The Zoning Administrator may approve a reduced parking permit for tandem parking for commercial and industrial uses provided the development requires 250 or more parking spaces, no more than a maximum of 20 percent of the total number of spaces are in tandem and an attendant is on duty during the hours the building is open for business.

D. *Low-income housing.* The Zoning Administrator may approve a reduced parking permit for the reduction in the number of parking spaces required for low- to moderate-income housing developments provided additional documents, covenants, deed restrictions, or other agreements as may be deemed necessary by the Zoning Administrator are executed.

E. *Landmarks and historic districts.* The Zoning Administrator may approve a reduced parking permit for the reduction in the number of parking spaces required for a designated landmark or a contributing structure within a designated historic district under the following circumstances:

   1. When an addition is proposed to a single-family home that is nonconforming due to the required number of parking spaces, no additional parking spaces shall be required for the addition of a bedroom, provided that the total

addition to the structure does not exceed more than 25 percent of the square footage of the existing structure or 250 square feet, whichever is greater, and that at least one covered parking space is provided on site. Only one such reduced parking permit may be permitted per designated structure.

2. When an addition is proposed to a multifamily structure that is nonconforming due to the required number of parking spaces, no new parking spaces shall be required, provided that the addition does not add more than one bedroom to each dwelling unit, the addition does not result in the addition of a new dwelling unit on the parcel and that at least one parking space is already provided on site per dwelling unit. Only one such reduced parking permit may be permitted per unit in a designated structure.

3. When an addition is proposed to a commercial or an industrial structure that is nonconforming due to the required number of parking spaces, no additional parking space shall be required, provided that the addition does not exceed 10 percent of the building's existing floor area. Only one such reduced parking permit may be permitted per designated commercial or industrial structure.

4. Commercial or industrial structures that change to a use which has more intensive parking standards than the current use may be permitted to reduce the required parking according to the following formula:

Total Required Parking Spaces After Change of Use	Percentage Reduction from Total Required Spaces
1 to 10	Up to 50%
11 to 20	Up to 25%
21 and over	Up to 10%

STRATEGY 2.1 ACHIEVING PLANNED DENSITY

Ashland, Oregon, Central Overlay District

18.30.030 Neighborhood Central Overlay—NM-C

A. *Permitted density.* The density shall be computed by dividing the total number of dwelling units by the acreage of the project, including land dedicated to the public. Fractional portions of the answer shall not apply towards the total density. Base density for the Neighborhood Central Overlay shall be 20 units per acre; however, units of less than 500 square feet of gross habitable area shall count as 0.75 units for the purposes of density calculations.

B. *Off-Street parking.* In all areas within the Neighborhood Central Overlay, all uses are not required to provide off-street parking or loading areas, except for residential uses where one space shall be provided per residential unit. All parking areas shall comply with the Off-Street Parking chapter and the Site Review chapter.

C. *Area, yard requirements.* There shall be no minimum lot area, lot coverage, front yard, side yard or rear yard requirement, except as required under the Off-Street Parking Chapter or where required by the Site Review Chapter.

D. *Solar access.* The solar setback shall not apply in the Neighborhood Central Overlay.

E. *Permitted uses.* The following uses are permitted in the NM-C overlay subject to conditions limiting the hours and impact of operation:

1. Residential uses, subject to the above density requirements

2. Home occupations

3. Parks and open spaces

4. Agriculture

5. Neighborhood-oriented retail sales and personal services, with each building limited to 3,500 square feet of total floor area

6. Professional offices, with each building limited to 3,500 square feet of total floor area

7. Restaurants

8. Manufacturing or assembly of items sold in a permitted use, provided such manufacturing or assembly occupies 600 square feet or less and is contiguous to the permitted retail outlet.

9. Basic utility providers, such as telephone or electric providers, with each building limited to 3,500 square feet of total floor area.

10. Community services, with each building to 3,500 square feet of total floor area

11. Churches or similar religious institutions, when the same such use is not located on a contiguous property, nor more than two such uses in a given overlay

12. Neighborhood clinics, with each building limited to 3,500 square feet of total floor area

F. *Conditional uses*
   1. Temporary Uses
   2. Public Parking Lots

STRATEGY 2.2. AND 2.3. ATTACHED UNITS

Richland, Washington, High-Density Residential, Small Lot Use District

The High-Density Residential, Small Lot Use District (R-2S) is a residential zone classification permitting higher density of population, encouraging small-lot development conducive to energy conservation and to other factors contributing to the production of affordable housing, and including the establishment of duplex dwellings and providing for these one- and two-family residences a high degree of protection from hazards, objectionable influences, building congestion and lack of light, air, and privacy. Certain essential and compatible public service facilities and institutions are permitted in this district. . . . Minimum lot requirements are:

(a) Minimum lot area for a detached one-family dwelling shall be 4,000 square feet;

(b) Minimum lot width for a detached one-family dwelling shall be 42 feet;

(c) Minimum lot area for a two-family dwelling shall be 7,000 square feet;

(d) Minimum lot width for a two-family dwelling shall be 64 feet;

(e) Minimum lot area for an attached one-family dwelling shall be 3,000 square feet; and

(f) Minimum lot width for an attached one-family dwelling shall be 30 feet.

Accessory Units Model Ordinance from State of Washington

<u>Model Accessory Dwelling Unit Ordinance Recommendations</u>

Washington State Department of Community, Trade, and Economic Development, January 1994

Definitions. An Accessory Dwelling Unit (ADU) is a habitable living unit that provides the basic requirements of shelter, heating, cooking, and sanitation. *[Comment. The Uniform Building Code (UBC) Sec. 1207 & 1208 lists minimum room sizes for an efficiency unit. The jurisdiction could set up maximum areas in the Standards and Criteria below, if it so desired.]*

Purpose and Intent

A. The installation of an ADU in new and existing single-family dwellings (hereinafter principal units) shall be allowed in single-family zones subject to specific development, design, and owner-occupancy standards.

B. The purpose of allowing ADUs is to:

1. provide homeowners with a means of obtaining, through tenants in either the ADU or the principal unit, rental income, companionship, security, and services;

2. add affordable units to the existing housing;

3. make housing units available to moderate-income people who might otherwise have difficulty finding homes within the (city/county);

4. develop housing units in single-family neighborhoods that are appropriate for people at a variety of stages in the life cycle; and

5. protect neighborhood stability, property values, and the single-family residential appearance of the neighborhood by ensuring that ADUs are installed under the conditions of this ordinance.

Standards and Criteria

A. ADUs shall meet the following standards and criteria:

1. The design and size of the ADU shall conform to all applicable standards in the building, plumbing, electrical, mechanical, fire, health, and any other applicable codes. When there are practical difficulties involved in carrying out the provisions of this ordinance, the (building official) may grant modifications for individual cases. *[Comment: Construction shall conform to all codes which are required for any new construction.]*

2. Certification by the (city/county) Health Department that the water supply and sewage disposal facilities are adequate for the projected number of residents must be provided to the building official. *[Comment: More applicable in rural areas for septic and wells. It is actually covered by No. 1 above.]*

3. Any additions to an existing building shall not exceed the allowable lot coverage or encroach into the existing setbacks. *[Comment: Planning ordinance already in place in most jurisdictions.]*

4. The ADU may be attached to, or detached from, the principal unit. *[Comment: Jurisdictions need to survey their existing housing stock and neighborhood standards to determine where and how ADUs would best fit their housing needs. This would allow the most diversity of choice and honor the uniqueness of each site.]*

5. Only one ADU may be created per residence in single-family zones. Multiple detached ADUs may be created in (agricultural) zones, if one of the occupants of each unit is employed by the property owner. *[Comment: The first sentence is to "maintain single-family appearance." The second sentence is appropriate in agricultural zones.]*

6. The property owner, which shall include title holders and contract purchasers, must occupy either the principal unit or the ADU as their permanent residence, but not both, for at least [enter number] months out of the year, and at no time receive rent for the owner-occupied unit. *[Comment: Owner-occupied units are better maintained, and therefore the neighborhood will be better maintained. If the owner has to live on site for more than six months out of the year, they could not own more than one ADU. This would eliminate speculators/developers from developing duplexes throughout an area under the guise of calling them ADUs.]*

7. An ADU may be developed in either an existing or a new residence. *[Comment: This would allow new home builders to plan ahead for "mother-in-law" type units and thus save money now and time and inconvenience later.]*

8. In no case shall an ADU be more than 40 percent of the building's total floor area, nor more than 800 square feet, nor less than 300 square feet, nor have more than two bedrooms, unless in the opinion of the [building official], a greater or lesser amount of floor area is warranted by the circumstances of the particular building. *[Comment: The existing structure, the lot size, or the jurisdiction will determine ADU's size.]*

9. The ADU shall be designed so that, to the degree reasonably feasible, the appearance of the building remains that of a single-family residence. *[Comment: To maintain single-family appearance. This is a subjective evaluation and unless specific design standards are adopted by the jurisdiction, this may be difficult to consistently apply.]*

10. The primary entrance to the ADU shall be located in such a manner as to be unobtrusive from the same view of the building which encompasses the entrance to the principal unit. *[Comment: The second entrance is located this way to maintain single-family appearance with an attached ADU. Less restrictive than "no second entry on the street side of the principal unit," but it allows for site restriction that may make a side or rear entry impossible.]*

11. One off-street parking space, in addition to that which is required by the ordinance for the underlying zone, shall be provided or as many spaces deemed necessary by the [building official] to accommodate the actual number of vehicles used by occupants of both the primary dwelling and the ADU. Parking spaces include garages, carports, or off-street areas reserved for vehicles. *[Comment: Parking requirements may vary from jurisdiction to jurisdiction depending on density of neighborhood, existing neighborhood standards, etc. Other parking options include more than one additional space, tandem parking, or allowing on-street parking.]*

12. In order to encourage the development of housing units for people with disabilities, the [building official] may allow reasonable deviation from the stated requirements to install features that facilitate accessibility. Such facilities shall be in conformance with the UBC. *[Comment: This is an accessibility issue.]*

Grandfathering

Option 1. ADUs created prior to [date] shall be registered with the [building official] for inclusion into the Certificate of Occupancy Program. Application for registration must contain the name of the owner, the address of the unit, the floor area of the two dwelling units, a plot plan of the property, evidence of the date of establishment of the unit, evidence of the use for the six-month period prior to the application for registration, and a signature of the owner. *[Comment: This provision would allow the building official to verify the compliance of the ADU to the codes and to require changes as necessary.]*

Option 2. Ignore. *[Comment: It would be difficult and very time consuming to determine under which codes the ADU was originally constructed.]*

Application Procedure

A. Application for a building permit for an ADU shall be made to the [building official] in accordance with the permit procedures established in Section [enter number] and shall include:

1. A letter of application from the owner(s) stating that the owner(s) shall occupy one of the dwelling units on the premises, except for bona fide temporary absences [for [enter number] months out of each year]. *[Comment: This is an owner-occupancy requirement. Limits the owner from "living" in several units at the same time.]*

2. The registration form or other forms as required by the [building official] shall be filed as a deed restriction with the [county] Department of Records and Elections to indicate the presence of the ADU, the requirement of owner-occupancy, and other standards for maintaining the unit as described above. *[Comment: This is for optional use if the owner-occupancy requirement is adopted.]*

3. The [building official] shall report annually to the [council] on ADU registration, number of units and distribution throughout the [city/county], average size of units, and number and type of complaint and enforcement-related actions. *[Comment: This is a local jurisdiction option. This provides a tracking mechanism on the number of ADUs to determine if changes to the ordinance are needed.]*

4. Cancellation of an ADU's registration may be accomplished by the owner filing a certificate with the [building official] for recording at the [city/county] Department of Records and Elections or may occur as a result of enforcement action.

5. This ordinance shall take effect and be in force five days after passage and legal publication. *[Comment: This is a local jurisdiction option.]*

STRATEGY 3.1. MIXED-USE BUILDINGS

Kennebunk, Maine, Provisions for Mixed-Use Development

Part D. Mixed Uses and Nonresidential Uses

Section 16. Mixed Residential and Commercial Uses. Residential and commercial uses may be combined on a single lot in any district, provided that:

A. The uses are only those allowed within the district in which the lot is located; and

B. Unless otherwise specifically stated within the district regulations, each of the uses shall individually meet the space and bulk standards set forth in the district; and

C. Unless otherwise specifically stated within the district regulations, each of the uses shall individually meet the off-street parking requirements of this article; and

D. Any signs comply with the standards for signs set forth in this article.

San Diego, California, Live/Work Units

Section 101.0570 — Live/Work Quarters (Lofts)

A. **Purpose and Intent**. The purpose of this Section is to provide for and make feasible the reuse of existing commercial and industrial buildings for joint live/work quarters as contemplated by Section 17958.11 of the Health and Safety Code. Live/work quarters in the City of San Diego are intended to be occupied by artists, artisans, and similarly situated individuals.

B. **Definitions**

1. *artist.* One whose works are subject to aesthetic criteria. An individual who practices one of the fine arts, who works in one of the performing arts or whose trade or profession requires a knowledge of design, drawing, painting, etc.

2. *artisan.* One who is skilled in an applied art; a craftsman.

3. *live/work quarters (loft).* An area comprised of one or more rooms or floors in a building originally designed for industrial or commercial occupancy which has been or will be remodeled or altered to include (1) cooking space and sanitary facilities and (2) working space reserved for persons residing therein.

C. **Development Criteria**

1. Subject to the provisions of Section 101.0570, live/work quarters shall be permitted in the City of San Diego in those areas designated on certain [maps] filed in the Office of the City Clerk.

2. Each live/work quarters shall be separated from other live/work quarters or other uses in the building and access to live/work quarters shall be provided only from common access areas, halls, or corridors.

3. Each live/work quarters shall have a separate access from other live/work quarters or other uses within the building.

4. Not over 33 percent of each live/work quarters shall be used or arranged for residential purposes such as a sleeping area, kitchen, bathroom, and closet areas. The minimum area of a live/work quarters shall be 750 square feet.

D. **Conditions of Approval**

1. For proper security, all exterior doors which provide access to live/work quarters shall remain locked at all times.

2. Access to each live/work quarters shall be clearly identified in order to provide for emergency services.

3. Persons other than residents of live/work quarters shall not be employed or permitted to work in that live/work quarters.

4. Live/work quarters shall not be used for mercantile, classroom instructional usage, storage of flammable liquids, or hazardous materials, welding or any open flame work, offices, or establishments with employees.

5. Live/work quarters shall be occupied and used only by an artist, artisan, or a similarly situated individual, or a family of which at least one member shall be an artist, artisan, or a similarly situated individual.

E. **Administration**

1. Requirements for Application
   a. Application for a live/work quarters permit shall be made in accordance with Section 111.0202. The application shall include a description of existing uses within the building where the proposed live/work quarters will be located and a legal description of the property.

2. Live/Work Quarters Permit Required
   a. No property shall be used for live/work quarters unless located within the area described in Section 101.0570(C)(1) and a live/work quarters permit has been obtained from the Development Services Director.

   b. The Development Services Director may approve or deny a live/ work quarters permit in accordance with "Process One." The permit shall be approved if the project meets the Development Criteria of Section 101.0570(C), and subject to the conditions of approval described in Section 101.0570(D).

3. Building permit required. Prior to the use of any building, or portion thereof, for live/ work quarters, a building permit shall be obtained from the Development Services Department. A copy of the application for a live/work quarters permit, approved by the Development Services Director, shall accompany the building permit application. The prevailing Uniform Building Code Regulations shall apply except as provided by code interpretations as shown in a Development Services Department Newsletter.

F. **Enforcement.** Any violations of the provisions of this ordinance or of any condition or requirement of any permit granted shall be resolved by the affected city department in accordance with adopted procedures in the San Diego Municipal Code.

STRATEGY 3.2. MIXED-USE NEIGHBORHOODS

San Diego, California, Institutional Overlay Zone for Neighborhoods

Section 101.0460 — Institutional Overlay Zone

A. **Purpose and Intent.** Institutions are considered a substantial public investment and a vital component within the fabric of a viable neighborhood. Neighborhoods depend upon institutions for the services they provide. Institutions contribute to a neighborhood's identity as well as to its character and general welfare. Institutions provide open space in the form of visual relief from monotonous single land uses and they provide for recreational and/or community facilities. Removal of an institutional use from a neighborhood may create adverse negative impacts. Therefore, it is the purpose of this overlay zone to preserve and enhance areas for institutional land uses until it is determined through a General Plan and/or a Community Plan amendment and a rezone that the appropriate long-term use of the site is not institutional in nature. It is intended to apply this overlay zone to publicly owned land designated for institutional purposes in community plans. Use of the property will be limited to institutional uses. Other uses as allowed by the underlying zone may be considered but only through a special use permit process. The special use permit may be approved if the proposed use of the site is in compliance with the adopted community, specific, or general plan including the text of the plan providing alternative land-use language.

B. **Application of the Institutional Overlay Zone.** The City Council . . . may apply the Institutional Overlay Zone applied to property if designated for institutional purposes on an adopted General Plan, community plan, or specific plan provided such land is owned by a governmental agency, other than a school or community college district.

C. **Institutional Uses**
   1. Institutional uses including but not limited to:
      a. Hospitals and medical service organizations
      b. Government owned and operated offices, public safety facilities, and libraries
      c. Park and recreational areas
      d. Cultural and community centers
      e. Museums
      f. Golf courses
   2. Those uses permitted by the underlying zone subject to the special use permit outlined in Paragraph E of this section.
   3. Joint uses (such as residential and a community facility) if the joint use would assist in maintaining the structure and the site for public use, subject to the special use permit outlined in Paragraph E of this section.
   4. Any other use, which the planning commission determines. . .to be similar in character to the uses enumerated in this section and consistent with the purpose and intent of this section. The Planning commission's determination shall be filed with the office of the city clerk.

D. **Development Regulations.** Demolition of the building or structure, or reuse of the building or structure to a use not listed in Paragraph C of this section, will require a special use permit obtained in accordance with the procedure set forth in Paragraph E of this section. In the case of destruction by fire, explosion, or act of God to the extent of over 50 percent of the fair-market value of the institutional structure, and in the case where the property owner does not wish to rebuild the structure for an institutional purpose, reuse of the site to a noninstitutional use may be allowed through a special use permit obtained in accordance with the procedures outlined in Paragraph E of this section. Other regulations as contained in the Municipal Code, including, but not limited to, the conditional use permit process, shall pertain to this section as well.

E. **Special Use Permit (SUP).** Within an Institutional Overlay Zone, no building shall be demolished, nor shall any building be constructed, nor shall any change in use occur, until a special use permit is obtained in accordance with the procedure set forth in this section, or a conditional use permit is obtained in accordance with the procedures set forth in Chapter X, Article 1, Division 5.

1. If a demolition is proposed, the following procedures shall precede consideration of the application for a special use permit:

    a. The request for demolition may be approved or denied by the City Council in accordance with "Process Five."

    b. The City Council shall consider whether:

        i. The property was duly offered to all appropriate public agencies in accordance with the regulations and restrictions of applicable State laws.

        ii. The existing structures are needed to meet a public need or contribute to the general welfare of the community. Determination of public need shall be made based on evidence presented by the applicant, including, but not limited to, the following showing that:

        iii. Availability of the site for purchase or lease was noticed in a citywide newspaper and any newspaper distributed in the affected community. Any and all responses to the notice shall be submitted with the application.

        iv. The Community Planning Committee and the community planning group for the area were notified of the availability of the site.

        v. The City of San Diego, Departments of Park and Recreation, Property and Planning, and the Mayor and City Council were notified of the availability of the site.

        vi. The County Department of Real Property and the school district governing the area were notified.

        Responses to the above notifications will be used to determine if the existing structures are needed to meet a public need.

    c. The City Council may approve the proposed demolition or delay the demolition for a period of 180 calendar days. If there is evidence that progress is being made, good cause is shown and that it appears that preservation may be completed within the time requested, the City Council may extend the period before which demolition can commence for a period not to exceed 180 calendar days.

2. After obtaining a demolition approval, or if such approval is not required, any proposed construction shall follow the procedure listed below:

    a. An application shall be submitted to the Development Services Department in accordance with Section 111.0202. The application shall include a site plan, grading plan, sections, elevations, a landscaping plan, and any other information the Development Services Director requests to assist in evaluating the proposal.

    b. The City Council may approve the application if the following findings of fact are made:

i. The proposed development is in conformance with the adopted General Plan, community plan, and/or specific plan that governs the site including the text of the plan that provides alternative land-use language.

ii. The proposed development conforms with the adjacent neighborhood land uses in terms of density, architectural design, scale, character, compatibility, and landscaping treatments.

iii. The proposed development will not be detrimental to the health, safety, and general welfare of persons residing or working in the area, and will not adversely affect other property in the vicinity.

iv. If joint uses are proposed, the uses shall not create excessive noise, traffic, or other negative impacts to the surrounding community.

c. If the findings are made, the City Council shall issue the special use permit. The decision of the Planning Commission may be appealed in accordance with the provisions of Section 101.0240. The special use permit shall be recorded in the office of the County Recorder of San Diego County.

F. **Exemptions from Special Use Permit.** The following circumstances would exempt a project from the requirements of the institutional special use permit:

1. Interior modifications to existing structures shall be exempt from the regulations of this overlay zone.

2. If a proposed development receives a community plan amendment to remove the institutional designation from the site, a special use permit would not be required.

3. If a rezone removing the Institutional Overlay Zone is approved, a special use permit would not be required.

4. If a proposed development receives a discretionary permit, such as a planned development or conditional use permit, a special use permit would not be required, but the findings of fact contained in this section would be required.

5. If a development is proposed on property with an existing conditional use permit, amendment to the existing conditional use permit reflecting the proposed changes would exempt the project from a special use permit, but the findings of fact contained in this section would be required.

6. If a proposed development currently requires a conditional use permit according to Chapter X, Division 5, of the Municipal Code, a special use permit would not be required, but the findings of fact as contained in this section would be required.

Kennebunk, Maine, Provisions for Mixed-Use Development

Part D. Mixed Uses and Nonresidential Uses

Section 16. Mixed Residential and Commercial Uses. Residential and commercial uses may be combined on a single lot in any district, provided that:

A. The uses are only those allowed within the district in which the lot is located; and

B. Unless otherwise specifically stated within the district regulations, each of the uses shall individually meet the space and bulk standards set forth in the district; and

C. Unless otherwise specifically stated within the district regulations, each of the uses shall individually meet the off-street parking requirements of this article; and

D. Any signs comply with the standards for signs set forth in this article.

Hermosa Beach, California, Standards for Neighborhood Commercial (C-1), Downtown Commercial (C-2), and General Commercial (C-3) Zones

17.26.010 General Provisions. In the C-zones, no building shall be erected, constructed, reconstructed, structurally altered, or shall any building or land be used for any purpose except as hereinafter specifically provided and allowed by this chapter.

17.26. 020 Specific Purposes

A. In addition to the general purposes listed in Chapter 17.02, the specific purposes of the commercial zones are to:

1. provide appropriately located areas consistent with the general plan for a full range of office, retail commercial, and service commercial uses needed by residents of, and visitors to, the city and region;

2. strengthen the city's economic base and also protect small businesses that serve city residents;

3. create suitable environments for various types of commercial and compatible residential uses, and protect them from the adverse effects of inharmonious uses;

4. minimize the impact of commercial development on adjacent residential districts;

5. ensure that the appearance and effects of commercial building and uses are harmonious with the character of the area in which they are located;

6. ensure the provision of adequate off-street parking and loading facilities;

7. provide sites for public and semi-public uses needed to complement commercial development or compatible with a commercial environment;

B. The additional purposes of each zone are as follows:

1. *C-1 Neighborhood Commercial Zone.* To provide sites for a mix of small local businesses appropriate for, and serving the daily needs of nearby residential neighborhoods; while establishing land-use regulations that prevent significant adverse effects on abutting residential uses.

2. *C-2 Downtown Commercial Zone.* To provide opportunities for a limited range of office, retail, and service commercial uses specifically appropriate for the scale and character of the downtown—resident and visitor serving pedestrian-oriented shopping/entertainment district.

3. *C-3 General Commercial Zone.* To provide opportunities for the full range of office, retail, and service businesses deemed suitable for the city, and appropriate for the Pacific Coast Highway and Aviation Boulevard commercial corridors, including business not appropriate for other zones because they attract heavy vehicular traffic or have specific adverse impacts.

17.26. 030 C-1, C-2, and C-3 Land-Use Regulations. In the following matrix, the letter "P" designates use classifications permitted in commercial zones. The letter "U" designates use classifications permitted by approval of a conditional use permit. Use classification not listed are prohibited. Section numbers listed under "see section" reference additional regulations located elsewhere in the zoning ordinance or this code. For definition of the listed uses, see Section 17.04.060.

C-1, C-2 and C-3 Zones, Land-Use Regulations

P = Permitted; - = Not Permitted; U = C.U.P. Required (See Chapter 17.40)

Use	C–1	C–2	C–3	See Section
Adult businesses	-	-	U	17.40.050
Adult paraphernalia, X-Rated uses and materials, limited to no more than 20% of stock-in-trade	U	U	U	17.40.060
Alcohol beverage establishments, on-sale	-	U	U	17.40.080
Alcohol beverage establishment, off-sale (closing at 11:00 p.m. or earlier)	P	P	P	

C-1, C-2 and C-3 Zones, Land-Use Regulations
P = Permitted; - = Not Permitted; U = C.U.P. Required (See Chapter 17.40)

Use	C–1	C–2	C–3	See Section
Alcohol beverage establishment, off-sale (open between 11:01 p.m. and 2:00 a.m.)	U	U	U	17.40.090
Animal hospitals	-	-	P	
Aquariums, sales and supplies of marine life	P	P	P	
Art/antiques/curios gallery or shop	P	P	P	
Audio/video equipment and supplies, sales and repair	P	P	P	
Bakery	P	P	P	
Banks and financial institutions	-	P	P	
Barber/beauty shop	P	P	P	
Billiard or pool halls	-	P	P	
Books/news/magazines, sales	P	P	P	
Bowling alley	-	-	P	
Brick and stone (ornamental)	-	-	P	
Bus station, not including terminal facilities	-	-	P	
Business schools	-	-	P	
Catering business	-	-	P	
Clinic, dental and/or medical	P	P	P	
Clothing and wearing apparel sales and service	P	P	P	
Clubs, private	-	P	P	
Convention hall	-	-	U	17.40.020
Copying and printing services and supplies	P	P	P	
Dancing, customer	-	P	P	
Day nursery, preschool	U	U	U	17.40.110
Department stores	-	-	P	
Detective agency	P	P	P	
Drugstore	P	P	P	
Entertainment, live	-	U	U	17.40.020
Equipment (household tools and lawn/garden equipment including small engines) rental, and repair, other than street vehicles	-	-	P	
Florist or plant shop	P	P	P	
Food and beverage market (maximum 4,000-square-foot floor area)	P	P	P	
Fortune tellers, psychics and astrologers	-	-	P	
Funeral homes, including mortuaries	-	P	P	

C-1, C-2 and C-3 Zones, Land-Use Regulations

P = Permitted; - = Not Permitted; U = C.U.P. Required (See Chapter 17.40)

Use	C–1	C–2	C–3	See Section
Furniture/furnishings, sales and display	-	P	P	
Game arcade, if five or more machines	-	-	U	17.40.020
Garden equipment, small, hand-operated, sales and rentals	-	P	P	
Gun shop	-	-	P	
Gymnasium/health and fitness center	-	P	P	
Hardware/home improvement store	-	P	P	
Hobby and craft supplies and service	P	P	P	
Hospitals, general, psychiatric out-patient only	-	-	U	17.40.020
Hotels, motels	-	P	P	
Household appliances/office equipment, sales and repair	-	P	P	
Instruments (professional and/or scientific), sales	P	P	P	
Interior decorating studio, store or shop	P	P	P	
Laboratories	-	P	P	
Laundry business and dry-cleaning (including self-service)	P	P	P	
Locksmith business	P	P	P	
Lumberyard, retail	-	-	P	
Massage therapy business	-	U	U	17.40.160
Messenger service	P	P	P	
Miniature golf course	-	-	P	
Monuments	-	-	P	
Motor vehicles and equipment, sales and service (including motorcycles, boats, nontractor trucks, RV's) sales/rental, new or used general repair, service, installation				
of parts and accessories	-	-	U	17.40.020
body repair and painting	-	-	U	17.40.020
service station	-	-	U	17.40.030
parts and accessories, retail sales	-	P	P	
car washes or (self-service car wash)	-	-	U	17.40.030
vehicle storage	-	-	U	17.40.020
Movie theaters	-	U	U	17.40.020
Museums	-	P	P	
Music academy	-	U	U	17.40.020
Musical instruments, retail and repair	-	P	P	
Nurseries	-	-	U	17.40.020
Offices, general	P	P	P	
Parcel delivery terminal	-	-	P	

C-1, C-2 and C-3 Zones, Land-Use Regulations

P = Permitted; - = Not Permitted; U = C.U.P. Required (See Chapter 17.40)

Use	C–1	C–2	C–3	See Section
Parking lots and /or structures	P	P	P	
Pet grooming, no overnight kennels	-	P	P	
Pet stores, including sale of pets	-	-	P	
Photo engraving business	-	-	P	
Photography (equipment sales and service, film processing, studio)	P	P	P	
Printing and or publishing business, commercial	-	P	P	
Radio and television stations	-	-	U	17.40.020
Recycling, large or small collection facility	-	-	U	17.40.130, 17.40.140
Residence; one or more apartments may be built above a commercial building	U	-	-	17.40.020
Restaurant, with drive-in, or drive-thru window, or with outdoor walk-up window on public right of way	-	U	U	17.40.020
Restaurant/cafe	P	P	P	
Restaurant/cafe with beer and wine or (on-sale alcohol beverage establishment)	U	U	U	17.40.080
Reverse vending machine(s)	U	U	U	17.40.120
Secondhand merchandise, retail sales	-	P	P	
Skating rink, ice or roller	-	-	P	
Snack bar/snack shop	P	P	P	
Sound score production facility	-	-	U	17.40.020
Sporting/recreational equipment sales, service, and rental	P	P	P	
Supermarkets	-	P	P	
Surfboard manufacturing	-	-	U	17.40.020
Ticket broker/sales	-	P	P	
Tobacco store	P	P	P	
Toy store	P	P	P	
Upholstering shop	-	-	P	
Wedding chapel, commercial	-	-	P	
Youth Hostel	-	U	U	17.40.150
Entertainment, special performances	-	U*	U*	
Outdoor merchandise display, temporary outside dining, in conjunction with special event	U*	U*	U*	17.26.050(D)
Parade, circus or carnival	-	U*	U*	

* Allowed by special permit by city council on public streets/right-of-way, pursuant to Section 12.12.070, and permitted by right on private property in conjunction with such a special permit.

17.26. 040 Similar Use Permitted. When a use is not specifically listed in this chapter, it shall be understood that the use is prohibited unless it is determined by the community development director that the use is similar to and not more objectionable than other uses listed.

It is further recognized that every conceivable use cannot be identified in this chapter, and anticipating that new uses will arise over time, this section authorizes the community development director to compare a proposed use and measure it against those listed for determining similarity. The director's determination shall not be final until confirmed by the city council as a consent calendar item on the council agenda following the director's determination.

In determination similarity the director shall make all of the following findings:

A. The proposed use shall meet the intent of, and be consistent with the goals, objectives and policies of the general plan;

B. The proposed use shall meet the stated purpose and general intent of the zone in which the use is proposed to be located;

C. The proposed use shall not adversely impact the public health, safety, and general welfare of the city's residents; and

D. The proposed use shall share characteristics common with, and not be of greater intensity, density or generate more environmental impact, than those uses listed in the zone in which it is to be located.

17.26. 050 Standards and Limitations

Every use permitted or maintained in C-zones shall be subject to the following:

A. *Parking.* Parking shall be provided as specified by Chapter 17.44.

B. *Enclosures.* All uses shall be conducted wholly within a building enclosed on all sides, except for the following:

1. Outdoor uses may be permitted by Conditional Use Permit for uses listed as stated in the permitted use list;

2. Commercial parking lot;

3. Uses incidental to a use conducted primarily within a building located on the premises; provided that such incidental uses are not conducted in whole or in part on sidewalks, public ways or within any required front or rear yard; and provided, further, that such incidental uses are of a type which cannot be economically or practically conducted within buildings. Where incidental uses are not conducted within a building, no part of the area devoted to the incidental uses shall be considered as part of the required parking facilities. All outdoor storage or activities shall be substantially screened from public visibility, public streets, parks or other public places, and properties;

4. Temporary outdoor merchandise display and outside dining in conjunction with a temporary outdoor event, such as a sidewalk sale, authorized by the City Council by special permit as set forth in Section 12.12.070.

5. Outdoor dining or seating located in front of a restaurant or snack shop located on Pier Avenue, authorized by an Encroachment Permit for use of the public right-of-way obtained pursuant to Section 12.16.090 of the Municipal Code, which may include sales and consumption of alcohol in outdoor dining areas in conjunction with a Conditional Use Permit for on-sale alcohol within the indoor premises of the restaurant, subject to approval of the State Alcoholic Beverage Control Department.

C. *Merchandise.* No merchandise shall be sold other than at retail. Sale of repossessed merchandise or secondhand merchandise taken in by the seller as a trade-in on new merchandise is permissible, provided that such sales are conducted on the premises where such merchandise was originally sold, or any successor locations.

D. *Signs.* Signs for this section are regulated by Section 17.50.140.

E. *Building height*
   1. In the C-1 zone, any building may have a maximum height of 30 feet.
   2. In the C-2 zone, no building shall exceed a maximum height of 30 feet.
   3. In the C-3 zone, no building shall exceed a maximum height of 35 feet.

F. *Front yard setback.* No lot need provide a front yard except as may be required by a precise plan.

G. *Alley setback.* Buildings shall conform with Section 17.44.130.

H. *Rear and Side Yard Setback Adjacent to Residential Zones*
   1. *C-3 Zone.* A minimum rear and/or side yard setback of eight feet shall be provided, and an additional two feet of setback shall be provided for each story over the first story for structures that abut residential zones, except where public rights-of-way, 20 feet or greater in width, separate the commercial zone from the residential zone.
   2. *C-1 and C-2 Zones.* A minimum rear and/or side yard setback of five feet shall be provided, except where public rights-of-way, 20 feet or greater in width, separate the commercial zone from the residential zone.
   3. *Existing buildings.* Existing commercial buildings that do not comply with the above setback requirement adjacent to residential zones shall not be considered "nonconforming buildings" under the terms of Chapter 17.52. Therefore, such buildings may be remodeled or expanded as long as any new constructions conforms with the above setback requirements.

I. *Landscaping adjacent to residential zones.* The required rear and/or side yard area shall be landscaped and provided with an automatic watering system. Size, quantity, and type of landscaping shall be subject to review and approval by the planning director. Landscaping shall be appropriately maintained, trimmed, and void of weeds.

Boca Raton, Florida, Neighborhood Convenience Business District

Chapter 28. Zoning

Article XI. Business And Commercial Districts

Division 2. Neighborhood Convenience Business District

Sec. 28-716. Short Title. This division shall be known and may be cited as the city NCB district ordinance.

Sec. 28-717. Purpose. The purpose of this division is to permit the location of certain types of retail stores and business uses on a limited basis in a residential neighborhood whenever it is found to be necessary and desirable for the public health, safety, morals, general welfare, and convenience.

Sec. 28-718. Permitted Uses. No building, structure, or land or part thereof shall be erected, altered, or used, in whole or in part, in NCB districts for other than one or more of the following specified uses:

A. Personal service shops

B. Coin-operated laundries and self-service cleaning and dyeing establishments, subject to the provisions of this Code

C. Business, professional, and governmental offices which do not involve the use and storage of fleet vehicles on the site

Sec. 28-719. Conditional uses. Conditional use approval may be requested by the owner of the property in NCB districts for the following uses in accordance with Division 4 of Article II:

A. Business schools, kindergartens, nursery schools, and child care and adult care centers subject to provisions of Section 28-1416 et seq.

B. Business, professional, and governmental offices which involve the use and storage of fleet vehicles on the site

C. Retail sales

D. Restaurants with table or counter service seating a maximum of 50 patrons

Cross reference(s)—Supplementary district regulations for child care, adult care, and other specialized care centers.

Sec. 28-720. Prohibited Uses. In addition to those uses disqualified under the provisions of section 28-718, the following uses are expressly prohibited in an NCB district:

A. The sale of alcoholic beverages other than wine and beer

B. Laundry, dry cleaning, and dyeing establishments other than self-service operations

C. Nightclubs and bars

D. Outdoor storage of motor vehicles, except as permitted herein

E. Outdoor storage of any kind

F. All uses not specifically permitted in Section 28-718 or allowed as a conditional approval in Section 28-719

Sec. 28-721. Conformance. It is recognized that the retail store and business uses which are permitted under this division will be in close proximity to established residential neighborhoods. It is mandatory that the operation and performance of all uses in an NCB district shall be subservient to and compatible with the peace and tranquility of a general residential environment. In addition to the excluded uses specified in section 28-720, no operations or activities shall be allowed in an NCB district which disturb or annoy the residential inhabitants of the surrounding area, including but not limited to any of the following:

A. The operation of any instrument or device which creates interference with radio or television reception

B. Outdoor displays of merchandise or articles for sale

C. The transacting of any business or activity on an outside or open-air basis

D. The burning of refuse or operation of any incinerator

E. Pole signs of any type

F. The emitting of smells, odors or aromas, including cooking odors

G. Outdoor storage of refuse except in authorized receptacles

H. The production of any vibration, smoke, dust, or fumes

I. The causing of any glare from outside lighting devices

J. Any operation or business activity occurring between the hours of 11:00 p.m. and 7:00 a.m.

K. Any loud, excessive, or unusual noise resulting from the business activity or operations conducted in the district, including noises caused by the performance of service functions such as deliveries from motor vehicles and garbage pickup service.

Sec. 28-722. Configuration of Land and Minimum Dimensions. Any tract of land for which an NCB district application is made shall contain sufficient width and depth to adequately accommodate its proposed use and design. A minimum width of 100 feet and a minimum depth of 100 feet are required for any such plot.

Sec. 28-723. Setback and Landscaping Requirements. All NCB districts are required to have setback areas and landscaping along the front or street boundary, the rear boundary and the side boundaries thereof in accordance with the following provisions. For the purpose of this section, building setbacks from all abutting residential districts shall be a minimum of 50 feet, and a wall which is a minimum of six feet in height and smoothly finished on both sides shall be located at the district boundary lines.

Sec. 28-724. Yards

A. *Front yard.* Every plot in an NCB district shall have front or street setbacks of not less than 25 feet which shall be landscaped. Within the landscaped area, no paving shall be permitted except for permissible driveways or sidewalks leading to buildings or structures located thereon.

B. Rear yard. Every plot shall have a rear boundary setback of not less than 50 feet. Where no wall is required, then the first five feet of the rear yard shall be landscaped.

C. *Side yard.* Every plot shall have five-foot landscaped side yards

D. *Landscaping.* All landscaping required herein shall be subject to the approval of the community appearance board.

Sec. 28-725. Building Height. No building or structure or part thereof in an NCB district shall be erected to a height exceeding 25 feet.

Sec. 28-726. Minimum Floor Area. No building or structure shall be erected in an NCB district which has a ground floor area of less than 3,000 square feet.

Sec. 28-727. Accessory Buildings. No accessory buildings or structures shall be erected or permitted in the NCB district.

STRATEGY 3.3. NEIGHBORHOOD COMMERCIAL DISTRICTS

Blacksburg, Virginia, Downtown Commercial District

Article III. District Standards

Division 14. Downtown Commercial District

Section 3140. Purpose. The Downtown Commercial district is the heart of the Town culturally, geographically, and historically. It lends the Town its small-town architecture, scale, and feel. It is intended to be a predominantly pedestrian area, catering to bicycle and pedestrian traffic with shops and storefronts close to the road; pedestrian-scale, wide walkways; street trees; and limited off-street parking, well screened. The history of the area is retained with preservation of historic structures and replication of style in additions and expansions. The core of the downtown exudes the vitality of the interaction of people and activities. Commercial opportunities include a diversity of specialty, retail services, cultural, recreation, entertainment activities, and public functions.

Section 3141. Permitted Uses

A. The following uses and structures are permitted by right subject to all other applicable requirements contained in this ordinance:

Residential
single family, detached

Civic
administrative services
community recreation
cultural services
day care center
educational facilities,
    primary/secondary
home for adults
life care facility
nursing home

open space
post office
public parks and recreational areas
religious assembly
safety services
shelter
utility services, minor

Office*
financial institutions (without
    drive-through)
general office
medical office

Commercial*

clinic
commercial indoor entertainment
commercial indoor amusement
communication services
consumer repair services
funeral home
neighborhood convenience store
parking facility
pawn shop
personal improvement services
personal services

restaurant, fast-food
restaurant, general
restaurant, small
retail sales
specialty shop
studio, fine arts
veterinary hospital/clinic

Miscellaneous

accessory structures

*Without external speakers only. Any use which incorporates an external speaker may be permitted only with a special use permit.

B. The following uses may be allowed with a Special Use Permit

Civic

club
utility services, major

hotel/motel
itinerant vendor

Commercial

automobile repair
bed & breakfast
commercial indoor recreation
gasoline station
grocery store

Office

financial institution (with drive-through)

Miscellaneous

broadcasting and communication tower

C. Residential uses shall be allowed by right only in the upper floors of a multistory building and in the basement of a structure within the Downtown Commercial zoning district. . . .

Section 3143. Site Development Standards

A. Each lot must abut a public street

B. Maximum residential density: 48 bedrooms per acre

C. Maximum structure height: 60 feet

D. Building facades shall maintain a consistent street edge, with the exception of passages for pedestrian access and drives to parking areas. The street elevation of principal structures shall have at least one street-oriented entrance and contain the principal windows of the structure.

E. All roof-top equipment shall be enclosed in building materials that match the structure or which are visually compatible with the structure.

F. Parking facilities shall be located behind the front building line. The administrator or town council may grant exceptions if necessary due to the shallow depth of a parcel, the location of existing mature trees, or other similar circumstances.

G. Automobile entrances to the site shall be minimized and placed in such a way as to maximize safety, maximize efficient traffic circulation, and minimize the impact on the surrounding area. A maximum of two curb cuts shall be allowed per street frontage. Factors including the number of existing curb cuts in the area, the potential for increased traffic hazards and congestion, and the number of travel lanes of the street that serves the site shall be used to determine the number of curb cuts permitted.

H. Sidewalk displays of retail merchandise are permitted, provided that:

1. at least five feet of clearance is maintained at the store front entrance for adequate and uncluttered pedestrian access;

2. the display is located against the building wall and does not extend more than three feet into the sidewalk; and

3. the display area does not exceed 75 percent of the length of the storefront.

I. All utility lines, electric, telephone, cable television lines, etc., shall be placed underground.

J. Parking facilities shall be located behind the front building line.

Section 3143. Downtown Building Design

A. This section applies to all new structures and to additions of 400 square feet or more to existing structures.

B. The use of contemporary interpretations of earlier design styles of surrounding structures in the Downtown Commercial District is encouraged, including characteristics such as scale; massing; roof shape; window size, shape, and spacing; and exterior materials.

C. The street elevation of principal structures shall have at least one street-oriented entrance and contain the principal windows of the structure, with the exception of structures in a courtyard style.

D. Site plans shall include drawings, renderings, or perspectives of a professional quality which illustrate the scale; massing; roof shape; window size, shape, and spacing; and exterior materials of the structure.

E. The Building Design Committee shall review the site plans and make recommendations to the applicant for amendments to achieve consistency with this Section. These recommendations are advisory only. It is not mandatory that the applicant comply with the recommendations of this committee.

Niskayuna, New York, Town Center Overlay District

Article VIIIA. Town Center Overlay District

Section 220-48.1. Purpose

A. The purpose of the Town Center Overlay District is to develop an identifiable center of the Town of Niskayuna with the Town Hall and county branch library as its nucleus. Its intent is to further define a sense of community and to promote a traditional architectural and visual environment deemed important as part of the town's comprehensive planning process. A fully realized Town Center concept will incorporate the elements of institutional, commercial, vehicular, and pedestrian environments into an integrated commercial and civic design which reflects the community focus of the town.

B. The town center concept is implemented by use of an overlay district which imposes additional criteria on the underlying zoning districts. The boundaries of the Town Center Overlay District are shown on the Zoning Map of the Town of Niskayuna.

Section 220-48.2. Objectives. In order to achieve the town center concept, the following objectives shall be realized:

A. Signs shall be of a scale, height, material, and illumination which reflect the traditional concepts being promoted in the Town Center.

B. The pedestrian environment in the Town Center is essential for developing the sense of community desired by the town. Amenities shall be provided in the Town Center to promote pedestrian usage.

C. Vehicular circulation and parking should be accommodated without impacting the pedestrian experience. Adequate measures shall be provided to reduce vehicular/pedestrian circulation conflicts.

D. The architectural character of new and renovated buildings should be harmonious with the traditional architectural styles of the Town Hall and County Library as focal points of the Town Center.

E. The size and scale of buildings in the Town Center should be complementary to a pedestrian environment. Buildings located near the perimeter of the Town Center should be designed to provide a harmonious transition between the commercial development and its residential neighbors.

Section 220-48.3. Applicability. In addition to the applicable regulations for the underlying zones contained elsewhere in this chapter, certain requirements shall apply to properties located within the Town Center Overlay District. All applications for new signs or modification or replacement of existing signs shall be subject to the requirements of Section 220-48.4 of this Article. All applications for site plan review as specified in Section 220-41 of this chapter shall be subject to Section 220-48.5. All applications for new building construction and building exterior renovations/modifications which require a building permit, with the exception of single-family dwellings and their accessory uses, shall be subject to Section 220-48.7.

A. Signs shall be of a scale, height, material, and illumination which reflect the traditional concepts being promoted in the Town Center.

B. The pedestrian environment in the Town Center is essential for developing the sense of community desired by the town. Amenities shall be provided in the Town Center to promote pedestrian usage.

C. Vehicular circulation and parking should be accommodated without impacting the pedestrian experience. Adequate measures shall be provided to reduce vehicular/pedestrian circulation conflicts.

D. The architectural character of new and renovated buildings should be harmonious with the traditional architectural styles of the Town Hall and County Library as focal points of the Town Center.

E. The size and scale of buildings in the Town Center should be complementary to a pedestrian environment. Buildings located near the perimeter of the Town Center should be designed to provide a harmonious transition between the commercial development and its residential neighbors.

Section 220-48.4. Signs

A. *Purpose.* The purpose of these standards is to promote signs which are visually compatible with their surroundings and which avoid inappropriate materials and design.

B. *Applicability.* At any time that there is a new sign or a modification or a replacement of an existing sign in the Town Center Overlay District, the following standards shall apply. These sign requirements shall be considered a supplement to those standards in Section 220-22. In all cases where there is a conflict, these standards shall take precedence over Section 220-22 standards in the Town Center Overlay District.

C. *Permitted signs.* The following signs shall be permitted in the Town Center Overlay District:

1. Freestanding monument (ground) signs limited to only public or private place identification, further limited to private sites of five or more acres. Freestanding signs shall not be utilized for individual businesses.

2. Facade s

3. Directional signs

4 Temporary signs

D. *Prohibited signs.* The following signs shall be prohibited in the Town Center Overlay District:

1. Moving signs	4. Pennants/ribbons/ logo flags	6. Neon signs
2. Flashing signs		7. Backlit canopies
3. Animated signs	5. Pylon signs	

E. Minimum performance criteria. The following performance standards shall apply to signs in the Town Center Overlay District:

1. *Materials*

   a. Monument signs shall be constructed with materials used in the main structure and shall be compatible with the area.

   b. Facade signs shall be made of wood or signboard, carved and/or sand-blasted and finished with gold leaf or paint stains. Uniform material shall be used for signs on buildings that are connected by common walls, located in a common plaza or otherwise associated as a single group.

   c. Directional signs shall be of materials compatible with facade signs.

   d. Temporary signs may be of cloth or vinyl plastic.

2. *Height.* Freestanding monument signs as permitted in Subsection C(1) of this section shall be no greater than eight feet in height above the finished grade.

3. *Size.* Freestanding monument signs as permitted in Subsection C(1) of this section shall have a maximum area of 50 square feet per sign face for the primary sign and 24 square feet per sign face for any secondary signs. Double-faced signs are permitted. For all other signs, the size standards specified in Section 220-22 and Schedule I for the underlying zoning district shall apply.

4. *Illumination.* Sign lighting should minimize glare and maintain the aesthetic character of the area.

   Therefore:

   a. Signs may not be internally lit.

   b. Raised-lettering signs may be backlit. All other signs shall be externally lit.

5. *Logo.* In the event that a picture logo is displayed on a sign, it shall be incorporated into the permitted sign area to comprise not more than 30 percent of the sign area. All colors associated with a logo, as defined in this chapter, may be permitted.

6. *Colors.* Except as provided in Subsection E(5) above, a maximum of three colors shall be utilized for a sign. Colors shall match or complement the predominant building color.

7. *Lettering.* A maximum of two lettering styles shall be permitted on signs, except that all lettering associated with a logo, as defined in this chapter, may be permitted.

8. *Setbacks.* Freestanding monument signs shall have a minimum setback of 10 feet from the right-of-way line and 10 feet from the side property line and shall be located in a manner that does not interfere with required minimum sight distance at driveways or intersections.

9. *Number of signs.* A maximum of one facade sign per use is permitted, except that a use fronting on two streets may have one sign for each building front. A maximum of one freestanding monument sign as described in Subsection C(1) of this section is permitted per driveway up to a maximum of three signs, except that for two or more signs, driveways must be separated by a minimum of 200 feet as measured center line to center line.

Section 220-48.5. Pedestrian and Streetscape Amenities

A. *Purpose.* The purpose of these standards is to promote the pedestrian environment in the Town Center Overlay District through the provision of appropriate amenities.

B. *Applicability.* The standards in this section are applicable to all actions proposed within the Town Center Overlay District which are subject to site plan review as specified in Section 220-41. In addition to the materials regularly submitted for site plan review, the following items shall be incorporated into plans and details for a project located in the Town Center Overlay District.

C. *Minimum performance criteria.* The following minimum performance criteria shall be utilized for site designs within the Town Center Overlay District. The Planning Board is authorized to consider variations in the criteria to allow for flexible design concept.

1. *Sidewalks*

    a. Sidewalks shall be constructed in accordance with the Sidewalk Plan and Section detail contained in. . .this chapter.

    b. Sidewalks to be dedicated to the town for public access shall be contained within appropriate rights-of-way. They shall be concrete and a minimum of five feet in width.

    c. Sidewalks outside the public right-of-way shall be privately owned and maintained. They may be comprised of concrete, pavers, or other materials acceptable to the Planning Board. They shall be a minimum of four feet in width.

2. *Bikeways.* Where a bikeway is required, it shall be designed in general accord with the Guide for Development of New Bicycle Facilities, published by the American Association of State Highway and Transportation Officials (AASHTO), most recent edition, and with the Town of Niskayuna Bikepath Standards.

3. *Lighting.* Lighting shall follow the Planning Board and Zoning Commission of the Town of Niskayuna Guidelines for Lighting of Outdoor Areas Under Site Plan Review.

    a. Lighting in public areas shall meet the style and specification requirements as shown in the Composite Street Amenities Exhibits contained [in this chapter]. In general, pole-mounted lighting shall not exceed a total height of 30 feet from finished grade to top of fixture in public rights-of-way and a total of 18 feet in other public areas.

    b. Lighting in private areas shall be consistent in style with that described for public areas. In general, pole-mounted lighting in private areas shall not exceed a total height of 18 feet from finished grade to top of fixtures.

    c. Light sources for public and private lighting shall be metal halide.

4. *Amenities.* Amenities shall be required and included on the landscape plan to be reviewed by the Planning Board as part of site plan review. The plan shall include, but not be limited to, benches, bikes racks, trash receptacles and recyclable receptacles. These amenities are to be provided on the private portion of the site plan and will be privately owned and maintained. Amenities are shown separately and on the Composite Street Amenities Exhibits detail [in this chapter].

5. *Parking.* Parking shall comply with the standards established in Section 220-19 of this chapter. Off-street parking should be designed to minimize traffic and utilize space through combined access. Screening shall be applied in the parking lot design along parcel boundaries in order to maintain an aesthetic quality. Acceptable screening materials include fencing, berms, and vegetation. Setbacks and signage for parking areas shall follow existing zoning regulations.

6. *Landscaping.* Landscaping shall be included on each site in order to maintain an aesthetic quality in the Town Center and to provide screening for parking, loading, and storage areas. Landscaping internal to the parking area as well as adjacent to it at property lines shall be considered in the overall parking lot design. Conceptual techniques are illustrated in the landscaping detail contained [in this chapter]. Plant materials shall be selected with respect to scale and allotted amount of space. In addition, although plant materials may be listed under one category, they may also

meet the requirements of another, depending on usage. A suggested plant list includes, but is not necessarily limited to, the following plant material. Salt-tolerant species for use along public rights-of-way or interior parking areas are identified by an asterisk.

a. Street trees:

Deciduous trees
   Acer platanoides (Norway maple); (high tolerance*)
   Acer saccharum (sugar maple)
   Gleditisia triacanthos inermis (thornless honey locust)
   Quercus borealis rubra (northern red oak); (high tolerance*)
   Ginkgo biloba (maidenhair tree)

Specimen trees
   Crataegus oxyacorntha pauli (Paul's scarlet hawthorn)
   Malus floribunda (Japanese flowering crab apple)
   Prunus sargentii (sargent cherry)
   Pyrus calleryana bradford (bradford pear)
   Tilia cordata (little leaf linden)
   Pruns pendula subhirtella (weeping Japanese cherry)

b. Screening material:

Coniferous trees
   Pinus nigra (Austrian pine) *(high tolerance)
   Pinus strobus (Eastern white pine)
   Pinus sylvestris (Scotch pine)
   Picea abies (Norway spruce)
   Thuja occidentalis (Eastern arborviatae)
   Tsuga Candensis (Canada hemlock)
   Picea pungens (Colorado blue spruce) *(high tolerance)

Deciduous shrubs
   Viburnum tomentosum (doublefile viburnum)
   Viburnum lentago (nannyberry viburnum)
   Cornus mas (cornelian cherry)
   Euonymus alatus (winged euonymus)
   Rosa rugosa (rugosa rose)
   Viburnum burkwoodii (burkwood viburnum)
   Viburnum dentatum (arrowwood viburnum)

Coniferous shrubs
   Juniperus chinensis (Chinese juniper)
   Pinus mugo (mugho pine)
   Taxus canadensis (Canada yew) *(high tolerance)

c. Ground cover:
   Hedera helix (English ivy)
   Vinca minor (common periwinkle)
   Juniperus horizontalis (creeping juniper)
   Cotoneaster horizontalis (rockspray cotoneaster)
   Pachysandra terminalis (pachysandra)

Section 220-48.6. Application Procedures

A. *Transmittal of application to the Planning Board.* As provided in Section 220-67F(3) of this chapter, the Zoning Enforcement Officer shall transmit one copy of the application for a zoning and building permit and all related material to the Planning Board as required by Section 220–41.

B. *Material to be submitted*

1. Applications subject to site plan review shall supplement the requirements of Section 220–43 with such information as the Planning Board may require to

promote understanding of the applicant's compliance with the minimum performance criteria of Sections 220–48.4 and 220–48.5.

2. In those instances where the application is for a building and zoning permit for a sign alone, the applicant shall provide a sign detail only showing location, size, lighting, color, materials, and design.

C. *Modifications and waivers.* The Planning Board may waive one or more of the specific requirements of this Article upon a showing by the applicant that the regulation imposes an undue hardship due to such factors as existing conditions, site topography, or site configuration. The Planning Board shall approve the minimum waiver necessary to allow the application to be approved. The applicant for any such waiver shall have the burden of showing that the proposed project with such waiver shall have a minimum negative effect on aesthetics and compatibility with neighborhood character.

Section 220–48.7. Architectural Review Standards

A. *Purpose.* The purpose of these standards is to achieve an integrated commercial design that provides an architectural and visual environment consistent with the town center concept.

B. *Applicability.* With the exception of single-family dwellings and their accessory uses, this Section is applicable to all new building construction and building exterior renovations/modifications which require a building permit.

C. *Minimum performance criteria.* In order to determine that new building construction or building exterior modifications contribute to a harmonious effect in the Town Center Overlay District and promote a cohesive architectural appearance, based on color, materials, and style, the following minimum performance criteria shall apply:

1. *Colors.* Colors utilized for building exteriors shall be compatible and shall visually reflect the traditional concept of the town center. Examples of incompatible colors include metallics, neons, and/or primary colors.

2. *Materials.* Traditional materials (masonry, wood and stone) are generally required in the Town Center; however, contemporary materials (glass, steel, concrete and plastic/vinyl siding) may be considered if they are treated in a manner complementary to the traditional concept of the Town Center architectural theme. Examples of incompatible materials include exposed concrete block, metal siding, and reflective glass.

3. *Mechanical equipment.* Mechanical equipment shall be screened with appropriate architectural treatments consistent with the materials listed in Subsection C(2) above.

4. *Architectural features and details*

   a. Exterior facades, including eaves, columns, pilasters, cornices, windows (and window surrounds), door balusters, canopies, fascias, and roofs, shall be proportionate with the building and consistent with the town center concept. The scale of new construction, including the arrangement of windows, doors and other openings within the building facade, shall be compatible with surrounding buildings in the Town Center Overlay District.

   b. Compatible finishes and colors shall relate to the town center concept as identified in Subsection C(1) above. Inappropriate contemporary materials which are deemed not to be consistent with or not to blend well with the traditional context of the town center concept are prohibited on building facades [see Subsection C(2) above]. To the extent practicable, accessory structures shall conform to the finishes and colors established for the principal building.

D. *Architectural Review Board*

1. *Duties.* The Architectural Review Board shall review all proposed building construction or building exterior modifications within the Town Center

Overlay District and make advisory recommendations to the Planning Board with respect to their consistency with the minimum performance criteria of Section 220-48.7C.

2. *Credentials.* The Architectural Review Board shall consist of five members appointed by the Town Board. Members shall include at least one architect and one additional design professional who shall be an architect, landscape architect, land-use planner, or engineer. Members shall be appointed for five years and serve in staggered terms.

E. *Application Procedures*

1. *Transmittal of application to Architectural Review Board.* In the Town Center Overlay District, the Zoning Enforcement Officer shall refer two copies of an application for a zoning and building permit for construction, renovation, and/or modification of a building exterior to the Planning Board, which shall transmit one copy of the application and related materials to the Architectural Review Board.

2. *Application material; material to be submitted.* Upon receipt of an application, the Architectural Review Board may require that the applicant submit such additional information as follows, which shall provide for understanding of the project's compliance with the minimum performance criteria of Section 220–48.7C above. Such materials shall be prepared by a licensed engineer, architect, surveyor, land-use planner or any combination thereof and shall constitute the architectural plan.

   a. Architectural elevations of buildings, specifying dimensions, and materials.

   b. Details of ornamentation which include, but are not limited to, windows, roofs, facades and other building features.

   c. A color rendering which depicts actual colors, textures and building scale.

   d. Samples of materials and colors of building components.

3. *Modification and waivers*

   a. The Architectural Review Board may require such additional information on the architectural plan that promotes further understanding of the applicant's compliance with the minimum performance criteria.

   b. The Architectural Review Board may, at its direction, judge that certain requirements of the architectural plan are not applicable in its review of an application and, therefore, may allow the applicant to submit only those elements which it deems necessary to its review of the particular application.

4. *Action on Application*

   a. Upon reaching its decision, but in no more than 45 days from receipt of a complete application, the Architectural Review Board shall provide its recommendation to the Planning Board with respect to project compliance with the minimum performance criteria.

   b. The Architectural Review Board shall provide its recommendations to the Planning Board on a copy of the architectural plan along with a written report supporting its recommendations.

   c. The Planning Board may accept the report of the Architectural Review Board as a condition of its approval of the architectural plan or, upon showing of undue hardship by the applicant, waive one or more of the specific recommendations of the Architectural Review Board. The Planning Board shall approve the minimum waiver necessary to allow the application to be approved. The applicant for any such waiver shall have the burden of showing that the proposed project with such waiver shall have minimum negative effect on aesthetics and compatibility with neighborhood character.

Santa Monica, California, Neighborhood Commercial Overlay District

9.04.08.40.010 Purpose. The N Overlay District is intended to protect and enhance concentrations of neighborhood commercial uses that are located in Districts other than the C2 District. The N Overlay District is intended to preserve and enhance the concentration of neighborhood commercial uses at the ground-floor street frontage while permitting new development to be built to the development standards for the underlying district, consistent with the goals, objectives, and policies of the General Plan.

9.04.08.40.020 Permitted Uses. The following convenience goods and service type uses shall be permitted in the N Overlay District, if conducted within an enclosed building, except where otherwise permitted:

A. Artist studios above the first floor

B. Barber or beauty shops

C. Child day care centers

D. Cleaners

E. General retail uses

F. Laundromats

G. Photocopy shops

H. Small appliance repair shops

I. Small appliance stores

J. Restaurants of 50 seats or less

K. Tailors

L. Accessory uses which are determined by the Zoning Administrator to be necessary and customarily associated with, and appropriate, incidental, and subordinate to, the principal permitted uses and which are consistent and not more disturbing or disruptive than permitted uses.

M. All uses permitted in the underlying zoning classification shall be permitted in the N District but shall not be located at the ground-floor street frontage unless with the use, at least 50 percent of the lineal front footage of buildings, structures, or parcels on the block (on both sides of the street) will contain uses permitted in subdivisions (A) through (L) of this Part.

N. Other uses determined by the Zoning Administrator to be similar to those listed above which are consistent and not more disruptive or disturbing than permitted uses.

9.04.08.40.030 Uses Subject to Performance Standards Permit

A. Shelters for the homeless

9.04.08.40.040 Conditionally Permitted Uses. The following uses may be permitted in the N Overlay District subject to the approval of a Conditional Use Permit:

A. All uses listed as Conditionally Permitted Uses in the C2 District or the underlying District may be permitted subject to the approval of a Conditional Use Permit.

9.04.08.40.050 Prohibited Uses

A. Rooftop parking on parcels directly abutting, or separated by an alley from, a residential district

B. Any use not specifically authorized

9.04.08.40.060 Property Development Standards. All property in the N Overlay District shall be developed in accordance with the same standards as those listed for the underlying zoning district except the following, if different:

Front yard. None, but all new development and new additions to the front portion of existing development must adhere to the build-to line requirements relative to the street's building facade line pursuant to the provisions of Section 9.04.10.02.050.

9.04.08.40.070 Architectural Review. All new construction, new additions to existing buildings, and any other exterior improvements that require issuance of a building permit shall be subject to architectural review pursuant to the provisions of Chapter 9.32 of this Article.

STRATEGY 4.1. MULTIMODAL STREETS

See the Eugene, Oregon, Street Standards under Strategy 1.5 (above)

STRATEGY 4.2. TRANSIT, BIKE, AND PEDESTRIAN CONNECTIVITY

State of New Jersey Model Site Plan Approval Ordinance For Station Area Overlay Zone (1994)

Pedestrian-way easements [10] feet wide, through the center of blocks more than 600 feet long, may be required by the approving agency in order to provide convenient pedestrian access to transit stops, a station, to shopping, or other community facilities.

Model Ordinance from Visions for a New American Dream by Anton Nelessen (Chicago: Planners Press 1995)

The street shall be designed to create blocks that are generally rectilinear in shape, a modified rectilinear shape, or another district geometric shape. Amorphously shaped blocks are generally discouraged, except where topographic or other conditions necessitate such a configuration. To the greatest extent possible, blocks shall be designed to have a maximum length of 480 feet. Lanes (alleys) shall be permitted to bisect blocks.

STRATEGY 4.3. TRANSIT-SUPPORTIVE DEVELOPMENT

[*Editor's Note: For numerous examples of ordinance and plan language, see* Creating Transit-Supportive Land-Use Regulations *by Marya Morris, PAS Report No. 466 (Chicago, Ill.: American Planning Association, December 1996)*]

Washington County, Oregon, Interim Light Rail Station Overlay District
381-10 Minimum Density Requirements

381-10.1 Residential

A. Notwithstanding any contrary density standard in an underlying residential district, including residential districts with a lesser maximum density (i.e., the R-6 and R-9 districts), the density of residential development shall be the greater of:

   (1) 75 percent of the allowed maximum density of an underlying residential district; or

   (2) 12 dwelling units per acre for that portion of the district located within 1,300 feet of the proposed site of the light rail transit station boundary, and nine dwelling units per acre for that portion of the district located beyond 1,300 feet from the proposed site of the light rail station boundary.

STRATEGY 5.1. AND 5.2 COMPATIBLY DESIGNED BUILDINGS

Olympia, Washington, Residential Mixed-Use District

The purpose of the mixed-use district is:

a) to preserve existing downtown housing and to ensure that high-density housing and mixed-use development are included in appropriate areas; the permitted commercial uses are intended to help preserve the residential use of the area through provision of personal services within walking distance of the residences;

b) to increase development intensity in this zone while providing an alternative to the creation of an exclusive residential zone; commercial development flexibility would be increased while meeting the housing objectives of the comprehensive plan;

c) to encourage the development of downtown housing in a wide range of types and prices and rent levels;

d) to integrate the RMU [residential mixed-use] zone with surrounding business and commercial zones by allowing small-scale commercial establishments that would serve both residents and walk-in trade from nearby offices;

e) to create a continuity of pedestrian-oriented streetscapes and activities through the zone; and

f) to permit development of a scale, height, and bulk that reinforces downtown's historic character, buildings, places and street layout.

STRATEGY 5.3 PEDESTRIAN-FRIENDLY STREETSCAPES (COMMERCIAL DISTRICTS)

Portland, Oregon, Standards for Big-Box Setbacks

Chapter 33.130. Commercial Zones

33.130.215 Setbacks. Alternative maximum setback option for large retailers

1. *Purpose.* The intent of these regulations is to allow deeper street setbacks for very large retail stores locating along transit streets or in pedestrian districts in exchange for a pedestrian- and transit-friendly main street type of development. These large retail sites can still be transit-supportive and pedestrian-friendly by placing smaller commercial buildings close to the street and by creating an internal circulation system that is similar to streets to separate the parking area into blocks. The intent is to encourage development that will, over time, form a pedestrian-friendly main street along the perimeter of the parking blocks.

2. *Regulation.* Buildings with at least 100,000 square feet of floor area in Retail Sales and Service uses are exempt from the maximum setback requirement. . .if all of the following are met.

   A. Other buildings on the site have ground-level walls within the maximum setback for at least 25 percent of the frontage on a transit street or streets in a pedestrian district. . . . These buildings must be constructed before or at the same time as the large retail store.

   B. *Internal circulation system.* An internal circulation system that meets the following standards must be provided.

      1. Internal accessways that are similar to streets must divide the site into parking areas that are no greater than 55,000 square feet;

      2. These accessways must connect to the transit street, or street in a pedestrian district, at least every 250 feet;

      3. Each internal accessway must have at least one auto travel lane, curbs, and sidewalks on both sides at least 10 feet wide;

      4. Along each internal accessway that intersects a transit street, the parking must be provided between both sidewalks and the auto travel lanes except

for within 75 feet of the transit street intersection, measured from the street lot line, where parking is not allowed;

5. Curb extensions that are at least the full depth of the parking must be provided, as shown in Figure 130–1, at the intersections of internal accessways that have parking.

Portland, Oregon, Ground-Floor Windows Treatment

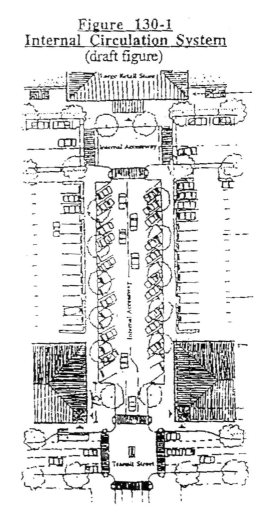

Figure 130-1
Internal Circulation System
(draft figure)

Chapter 33.218. Community Design Standards

33.218.140. Standards for All Structures in the RH, RX, C and E Zones

A. *Ground-floor windows.* Street-facing elevations must meet the Ground-Floor Windows Standards of the base CX zone. As an alternative to providing ground-floor windows, proposals in E zones may provide public art if the following conditions are met:

1. The area of the ground-level wall that is covered by the art must be equal to the area of window that would have been required;

2. The artist and the specific work or works of art must be approved by the Portland Regional Arts and Cultural Council; and

3. The art must be composed of permanent materials permanently affixed to the building. Acceptable permanent materials include metal, glass, stone and fired ceramics.

B. *Distinct ground floor.* This standard applies to buildings that have any floor area in nonresidential uses. The ground level of the primary structure must be visually distinct from upper stories. This separation may be provided by:

1. A cornice above the ground level;

2. An arcade;

3. Changes in material or texture; or

4. A row of clerestory windows on the building's street facing elevation.

Chapter 33.130. Commercial Zones

33.130.230 Ground-Floor Windows

A. *Purpose.* In the C zones, blank walls on the ground level of buildings are limited in order to:

- provide a pleasant, rich, and diverse pedestrian experience by connecting activities occurring within a structure to adjacent sidewalk areas;

- encourage continuity of retail and service uses;

- encourage surveillance opportunities by restricting fortress-like facades at street level; and

- avoid a monotonous pedestrian environment.

B. *Required amounts of window area*

1. In CN1 and 2, CO1 and 2, CM, CS, and CG zones, exterior walls on the ground level which are 20 feet or closer to the street lot line must meet the general window standard in Paragraph 3 below. However, on corner lots, the general standard must be met on one street frontage only. The general standard must be met on the street that has the highest street classification according to the Arterial Streets Classifications and Policies. On the other street(s), the requirement is one-half of the general standard. If two or more streets have the same highest classification, then the applicant may choose on which street to meet the general standard.

2. In CX zone, exterior walls on the ground level which face a street lot line, sidewalk, plaza, or other public open space or right-of-way must meet the general window standard in Paragraph 3. below.

3. *General standard.* The windows must be at least 50 percent of the length and 25 percent of the ground-level wall area. Ground-level wall areas include all exterior wall areas up to nine feet above the finished grade. The requirement does not apply to the walls of residential units or to parking structures when set back at least five feet and landscaped to at least the L2 standard.

C. *Qualifying window features.* Required window areas must be either windows that allow views into working areas or lobbies, pedestrian entrances, or display windows set into the wall. Display cases attached to the outside wall do not qualify. The bottom of the windows must be no more than four feet above the adjacent exterior grade.

D. *Adjustments.* Public art may be considered for adjustments to the ground-floor window provision. In all cases, the Metropolitan Arts Commission will review the application to determine whether public art is appropriate at the location, taking into account the scale and character of the building and area. The budget, selection process, final artwork, and installation must follow the guidelines of the Metropolitan Arts Commission and must be approved by the Metropolitan Arts Commission. Covenants will be required, following the regulations of Section 33.700.060, Covenants with the City, to ensure the installation, preservation, maintenance, and replacement of the public art.

Blacksburg, Virginia, Old Town Residential District

Article III. District Standards

Division 6. Old Town Residential (OTR) District

Section 3060. Purpose. The Old Town Residential district is created in recognition that those areas adjacent to campus and the downtown are experiencing pressures for transition to commercial or high-density residential use. These areas are the historic heart of the Town and lend much of its small-town character and unique architecture and pattern. The Old Town Residential District is intended to retain and protect that character while allowing broad special uses which ease the transition from commercial and campus to residential. The district is designed for a low- and medium-density residential base, with small-scale office, commercial, and retail uses in renovated or replicated housing, a dynamic mix of uses linked by a common historic residential character.

Section 3061. Permitted Uses

A. The following uses are permitted by right in the OTR, Old Town Residential District:

Residential
single family, detached
home occupations

Civic
community recreation
open space
public recreation
utility services, minor

Miscellaneous
accessory structures

B. The following uses are allowed only by Special Use Permit in the OTR, Old Town Residential District:

Residential
boarding house
multifamily dwelling
single family, attached
two-family dwelling
townhouse

life care facility
post office
religious assembly
safety services
shelter
utility services, major

Civic
administrative services
club
cultural services
day care center
educational facilities,
    college/university
educational facilities,
    primary/secondary
family day care home
home for adults

Commercial
bed & breakfast
clinic
parking facility
restaurant, small
specialty shops
studio, fine arts

Office
general office
medical office

Section 3062. Site Development Regulations

A. Minimum lot requirements

    1. Lot area: 7,500 square feet, except townhouses

    2. Lot frontage 40 feet

B. Maximum density: 15 bedrooms per acre, except single-unit residential

C. Minimum setback requirements

    1. Front yard: 20 feet

    2. Side yard: 7 feet, except on corner lots, a side yard facing the street shall be 20 feet or more

    3. Rear yard: 25 feet

D. Maximum height of structures, except church spires, belfries, cupolas, monuments, water towers, chimneys, flues, flagpoles, television antennae, and radio aerials are exempt: 35 feet; or 45 feet with an additional one-foot setback per foot of additional height

E. Maximum coverage:

    1. Lot coverage: 50%

    2. Floor area ratio: 0.30

F. The maximum dwelling unit occupancy shall be a family, plus two persons unrelated to the family; or no more than four unrelated persons.

G. All utility lines, electric, telephone, cable television lines, etc., shall be placed underground.

Portland, Oregon, Standards For Attached Garages

Section 33.295. Community Design Standards. Standards for Primary and Attached Structures in Single-Dwelling Zones

A. *Attached garages.* When parking is provided in a garage attached to the primary structure, and garage doors face a street, the following standards must be met:

    1. The garage must not be more than 40 percent of the length of the building frontage or eight feet long, whichever is greater.

    2. The front of the garage can be no closer to the front lot line than the front facade of the house;

    3. Garage doors may be no more than 75 square feet in area; and

    4. There may be no more than two individual garage doors.

STRATEGY 5.5. QUALITY ARCHITECTURAL DESIGN

[Editor's Note: No ordinance or plan language was offered in the original Oregon report, and the research department staff at APA also was unable to find any "regulation" that would encourage quality design by offering density bonuses. In keeping with the APA principle that a community's citizens should determine the architectural character of new development in order to enhance or preserve the community character, we recommend that interested readers consult Design Review *by Mark Hinshaw, PAS Report No. 454 (Chicago, Ill.: American Planning Association, February 1995), which describes the design review process. We encourage communities seeking to create quality architectural design to follow the process as it is described in that report.]*